PRAGMATISM
Its Sources and Prospects

PRAGMATISM
ITS SOURCES AND PROSPECTS

EDITED BY
ROBERT J. MULVANEY
AND
PHILIP M. ZELTNER

UNIVERSITY OF SOUTH CAROLINA PRESS

Copyright © University of South Carolina 1981
First Edition

Published in Columbia, S.C., by the
University of South Carolina Press, 1981

The essay "From Cynicism to Amelioration: Strategies for a Cultural Pedagogy" is reprinted by permission of New York University Press from *The Culture of Experience: Philosophical Essays in the American Grain* by John J. McDermott, ©1976 by New York University.

Manufactured in the United States of America

Library of Congress Cataloging in Publication Data
Main entry under title:

Pragmatism, its sources and prospects.

    Papers from a symposium held at the University of South Carolina, Oct. 31-Nov. 1, 1975.
    Includes index.
    1. Pragmatism—Congresses. 2. United States—Civilization—Congresses. 3. Philosophy, American—Congresses. I. Mulvaney, Robert J. II. Zeltner, Philip M.
B832.P76   144;.3   80-26475
ISBN 0-87249-404-7

CONTENTS

Preface   vii

Pragmatism: A Reinterpretation of the Origins and
    Consequences   1
    H.S. Thayer

The Pragmatists' Place in Empiricism   21
    W.V. Quine

Pragmatism and the Importance of Being Earnest   41
    Ernest Gellner

From Cynicism to Amelioration: Strategies for a
    Cultural Pedagogy   67
    John J. McDermott

Philosophy and Moral Values: The Pragmatic Analysis   97
    James Gouinlock

Index   121

PREFACE

THIS VOLUME CONTAINS THE PRINCIPAL PAPERS read at a symposium entitled "Pragmatism, its Sources and Prospects" held at the University of South Carolina on October 31-November 1, 1975. Intentionally coincident with the nation's Bicentennial celebration, the symposium was designed to explore some aspects of a philosophical movement uniquely and perhaps characteristically associated with American experience itself. No attempt was made to be exhaustive in the choice of topics. Indeed, given the complexity and richness of the pragmatic movement, such an effort would surely be frustrated. Rather, our planning was dominated by a desire to focus on certain delimited themes, such as the diversity of the movement and its historical links with American culture and thought. In addition, and without ignoring attention to negative estimates of its significance and consistency, we wished to suggest some possibilities of contemporary topical relevance, and to foretell the movement's likely consequences for the future of American philosophy.

This preface is not intended to be a full-scale introduction to the papers contained within. But one or two remarks on the specific topics and symposiasts chosen may be appropriate. One primary aim in conceiving the symposium was historical. The historical dimension tends to be less emphasized in modern philosophy, and there are precise and sound reasons for putting it at the second rank in philosophical analysis and speculation. But the peculiar rootedness of pragmatism, not only in the history of American philosophy, but even more significantly, in the wider and less definable areas of American culture and experience, is an unavoidable fact of the movement. It is scarcely possible to understand "pragmatism" without understanding "American" as well. In abstraction from this larger historical context, the movement is largely unintelligible. It was es-

Preface

sential, then, to lead off our examination of pragmatism with a consideration of this vital relationship. Our choice for presenting this section was the eminent historian of pragmatism, Professor H. S. Thayer, of the City University of New York, whose *Meaning and Action: A Study of American Pragmatism* remains the finest analysis we have of the main figures and themes of the movement. Thayer's contribution to this volume combines nicely the analysis proper to the critical philosopher with the discipline of the intellectual historian, both of which are so essential to the understanding of pragmatic thought.

The influence of pragmatism on institutional and cultural forms of life in this country has been so marked that its relevance to more theoretical philosophical concerns, particularly in the theory of knowledge, has tended to be underemphasized. An easy characterization of American thought, especially given the professional specializations of academic philosophy, might relegate pragmatism to a less rigorous, practical philosophy of life, didactic, rhetorical, scarcely distinguishable from journalism or popular psychology. But this polarization of hard-headed analytic philosophy on the one hand, and easy-going armchair philosophy on the other, is inadequate when applied to classic pragmatism. The continuity of technical and abstract theoretical questions with human life, personal and public, has been a perennial theme of pragmatic philosophy. To illustrate one aspect of this phenomenon, we included in our symposium, and present here, the distinguished Harvard philosopher and logician, Professor W. V. Quine, whose thought illustrates vividly the interface between modern analytic thought and certain positions in the pragmatism of men like Peirce and Lewis. Pragmatism has been an inclusive, eclectic, philosophically omnivorous movement in the history of thought, like the melting-pot culture which fostered it. Quine, in investigating the empirical element in pragmatic thought, invites further consideration of the deeper relational aspects of pragmatism, and of modern American philosophy in general.

The inclusion of Quine in a symposium on pragmatism will initially surprise many readers. One man who would not be surprised is Professor Ernest Gellner of the London School of Economics.

Preface

Late in our planning of the symposium, his piece "W. V. Quine, the Last Pragmatist" appeared in the *Times Literary Supplement* (July 25, 1975). Taking a kind of pragmatic advantage of the situation, we invited Gellner to continue his critical assessment both of Quine and of the pragmatic movement itself. Gellner is as much at home in the social sciences as he is in philosophy, and brings to his literate and urbane treatment of pragmatism the tools of cultural anthropology as well as of technical philosophy. This approach is at once unusually provocative, and peculiarly suitable to dealing with a movement of thought so closely intertwined with the character of a people.

It remains in the more practical areas of philosophy, areas such as social, political, and educational philosophy, that pragmatism has made its greatest impact. Whether this influence will continue into the future remains a large question. The two concluding papers focus on cultural and moral questions, both under the clear influence of John Dewey. In the first, one of America's most original cultural and social philosophers, Professor John McDermott, formerly of Queens College (CUNY) and presently chairman of the Department of Philosophy at Texas A & M, boldly defends a pragmatic and liberal social theory in the face of two of its most ardent critics from the left, Norman O. Brown and Herbert Marcuse. The liberal and pragmatic centrism of John Dewey can mediate, he argues, the extremist antinomies of recent political and cultural theory. The viability of McDermott's suggestion follows from the conviction that Dewey's thought, founded in the bedrock of modern scientific liberalism, is progressive and meliorist, but profoundly skeptical of eschatologies and ultimate solutions. It is more than a theory that is at issue, but a way of life, a "cultural pedagogy," to use McDermott's trenchant phrase.

Dewey's thought can also play the same mediating role in the larger task of developing a theoretical base for the moral enterprise itself. In our final paper, Professor James Gouinlock of Emory University, author of one of the most penetrating recent analyses of John Dewey's moral philosophy, *John Dewey's Philosophy of Value*, examines some of the assumptions in the recent and continuing dispute between John Rawls and Robert Nozick. These two men, more than any in recent years, have renewed the concept of a public philosophy, and it is appropriate that a pragmatic critique be forthcoming. Gouinlock criticizes both, not so much on the substantive suggestions made by each, as on the conception of practical philosophy underlying each position. Dewey can teach us much, he argues, on the precise role the philosopher can be expected to play in the resolution of social and political problems.

Pragmatism in its various forms cannot be considered a neat system of thought. Textured, open, "ragged at the edges," it defies simple analysis and compartmentalization. Perhaps this is one of the reasons why, in Thayer's words, "it has never been an entirely respectable form of thought." In its defense, it may be argued that experience itself will not be pigeon-holed, and that a philosophy of experience must be expected to be untidy. But the critic may legitimately point to this as a cop-out, a dereliction of the hardheaded, but necessary, duty of precise logical analysis. The papers in this volume will not resolve this conflict. Rather they are intended, by drawing upon a variety of philosophical tempers, to say nothing of psychological and literary styles, to heighten the sense of complexity and of ambiguity one finds in the pragmatic tradition. Pragmatism has been pluralistic, holding little that is philosophical alien to it. The adequacy of this omnivorousness, both in the truthful representation of things as they are and in the precise expression of words to describe those things, is the ancient question pragmatism raises for us once again.

PRAGMATISM:
A REINTERPRETATION OF THE ORIGINS AND CONSEQUENCES

H. S. THAYER

IT IS ALTOGETHER APPROPRIATE AT THIS TIME—Anno 1975—to celebrate the birth of pragmatism which made its entrance into the world just about one hundred years ago. A century is not very long as the life of philosophies is measured. After all, we continue to study the thoughts of philosophers who flourished twenty-five hundred years ago. Still, we may celebrate this one-hundred-year-old event in American philosophy in a manner fitting the occasion: namely, by some critical reflections on the circumstances of its birth and existence, some scrutiny of its leading ideas and tendencies, and some estimation of its merits. Criticism is recognition and critical recognition, even contention, is the breath of life in philosophy.

As a contribution to this subject, my reflections will be twofold. First, I will propose a hypothesis for enabling us to understand and appreciate the origins of pragmatism—and especially the complexity and scope of those origins. Second, I hope to suggest what might be regarded as of permanent value and interest in the legacy of pragmatism.

Critics of pragmatism used to explain it for us as a philosophy reflecting American commercialism and imperialism in government and business. The explanation perhaps does not need notice these days, nor examination: but it has had a persistent and wide appeal. And there is in popular idiom the word 'pragmatism' having the sense of the business ethos, of "getting things done," "getting practical results," and unprincipled expediency. A particularly curious feature of this sociological explanation of pragmatism, however, is its rendering inexplicable the fact that the major philosophers of pragmatism—Peirce, James, Dewey—have never been popular or received as sages in those very circles of power and industry for whom they were the alleged spokesmen. The great organs of public opinion, the soliloquizing of men of power, have not invoked James or Dewey as sources of inspiration or wisdom; Aristotle, Christ, St. Thomas—even Santayana—have had more esteemed roles in this respect. Even when pragmatism dominated academic philosophy in the early 1920s, and even in its revival these days, it has never been an entirely respectable form of thought. There are reasons for this. Pragmatism in America has largely been allied with progressive and reform tendencies, often critical, sometimes constructive. The more important fact is that pragmatism is not a philosophy in which to find solace, in which to find a defense of power or the status quo, or in which to find answers at all. It was conceived and proposed, rather, as a way of clarifying questions and a method for finding answers.

I.

When William James made pragmatism famous in his California address of 1898, "Philosophical Conceptions and Practical Results," he stated his sources. He credited the essential idea to Peirce: the *principle* of pragmatism he called it (or "maxim," as Peirce called it). He said he heard Peirce enunciate the principle "at Cambridge in the early '70's."[1] This was probably in the meetings of the "Metaphysical Club" in Cambridge (although the exact origin of the term and of the club is still uncertain). James also referred to Peirce's now-classic paper in 1878, "How to Make Our Ideas Clear," in which the principle is stated. James remarked concerning Peirce's principle: "It lay entirely unnoticed by any one for twenty years, until I, in an address before Professor Howison's philosophical union at the University of California, brought it forward again and made a special application of it to religion. By that time (1898) the times seemed ripe for its reception."[2]

Such are the historical outlines.

Peirce argued that one compelling factor in the fixing of our beliefs is the social impulse. The trouble with sheer tenacity, stubbornly resolving to believe what we believe at all cost, is the cost. As he says, the method of tenacity is accompanied by brilliant unlasting success. We become aware of coercive factors external to beliefs; and among these are other persons entertaining at times beliefs incompatible with our own. This is a source of dissatisfaction.

We thus want our beliefs to conform to "some *one* thing," some authenticating condition. He called this condition our conception of *reality*. Beliefs that bear a certain relation to reality are true; and these are beliefs that "would be the same for every person if inquiry were sufficiently persisted in." In this way the social impulse is fulfilled, only and finally, in the practice of the scientific method of settling belief.

Peirce's discussion of the emergence of the scientific method, in the well-known paper, "The Fixation of Belief,"[3] to which I have been alluding, treats it almost as an evolutionary development from more primitive forms—or methods—whose adaptation is due to its yield of maximum success and satisfaction in the human struggle to resolve doubt and attain belief.

In the development and practice of the method, as Peirce describes it, notions of meaning and truth play important and interdependent roles. To determine the truth of our beliefs we require a way of determining their meaning; and their meaning (or an important part of it) is what they purport to be true of, what they lead to in experience. The coalescence of truth and meaning is conspicuous in some of James's explanations of "the pragmatic method." It is, he says, an attempt "to interpret each notion by tracing its respective consequences. What difference would it practically make to any one if this notion rather than that notion were true?"[4] Roughly, to get at meaning we focus on truth and derivable consequences; to get at truth we focus on meaning and derivable consequences. Peirce thought of pragmatism as a theory of meaning, or a method for explicating meaning; James thought of it as a theory of meaning and of truth. Given the close interrelation of pragmatic meaning and truth, both views were right.

Peirce thought that philosophy and science had a common future and were kindred efforts in the expression of an evolving cosmic reasonableness. He often refers to pragmatism as an accepted procedure in the sciences. James follows him in this respect, although extending the application of pragmatism to religious issues. So construed as a method of critical clarification exemplified in the sciences, pragmatism is a reflection upon already-existing procedures, not a recommendation for scientific practice. But the question is: For whom is the recommended remedial method of clarification intended: More precisely, what intellectual forms and activities in American experience in the late nineteenth century appeared to generate the need for pragmatic clarification of ideas? Granted, clarity is a good thing; but why this special philosophical concentration on it in the 1870s?

There are, I think, two answers. There is first the fact that the Cambridge pragmatists were schooled in European thought and reared in the various traditions of transcendentalism, Scottish Realism, Kantian and Hegelian idealism, British empiricism (especially of the Mills), and the new evolutionary doctrines of Darwinism and Spencer. In this milieu, as the members of the Metaphysical Club discussed philosophical issues of current interest, pragmatism emerged as a useful technique for the clarification and analysis of technical problems. The problems seem to have been centered in questions of the nature of belief, rational conduct, and the evolutionary character of reality. This is the now-familiar aspect of the academic history of pragmatism, due for the most part to accounts that Peirce has left us, which historians have studied and continue to explore and illuminate. But there were also broader influential forces and currents in American culture at the time that could not have entirely failed to affect the philosophizing of the members of the club. This wider social context is one of unusual diversity and tensions and powerful divisions of interest. The pragmatists' conception of the function of thought as productive of stability and satisfaction or restoration of belief of inquiry as generated from conditions of tension and irritation, and of belief as a kind of betting and investment in action on the future, reflect something of the character of the wider historical context. Thus we come to the other, somewhat neglected part of the history of pragmatism concerning which something should be said.

Ever since the nineteenth century began, it has been characterized as the Century of Progress. There is abundant testimony from those who lived in it—or in the most comfortable centers of it—that the century promised unlimited prosperity and growth. "Progress" and "growth" are ubiquitous terms in nineteenth-century discourse. At the very dawn of the century, Wordsworth produced the *Prelude*, the autobiographical poem, on "the origin and progress of his own powers," and alternatively titling it prophetically: "Growth of a Poet's Mind." At the very close of the century, Charles Peirce commented:

> As this Century is drawing to a close, it is interesting to pause and look about us and to ask ourselves in what great questions science is now most interested. The answer must be that *the* question that everybody is now asking, in metaphysics, in the theory of reasoning, in psychology, in general history, in philology, in sociology, in astronomy, perhaps even in molecular physics, is the question *How things grow*.[5]

That things grow there seemed no doubt. The little word 'growth' is big with nineteenth-century preoccupations; they range from mathematical analysis of continuity, to the evolution of living forms, to business organizations and American cities.

This same century was the offspring of eighteenth-century enlightenment. But the enlightened mind and its rational ideals had found a powerful new body in which to work—the body of industry. Each age acquires its mother tongue from its predecessor. The nineteenth-century idea of progress as articulated by American intellectuals, businessmen, and politicians in theological academies and civic organizations had been enunciated earlier by several influential European thinkers. Condorcet, in the essay on *The History of the Progress of the Human Understanding*, set forth the idea of unlimited and accelerated human progress and perfectibility. This appeared in 1795, was received largely by French socialists and British utilitarians, and one year later was published in Philadelphia. Joseph Priestley and William Godwin were read and studied. From 1830 to 1840 Jeremy Bentham's writings were published in the United States. His influence not only took the form of active disciples, one of whom was Robert Owen, but the concept of *utility* appeared also to the rising industrial and middle class as one in which the idea and realization of progress and growth could be measured. The idea of progress was felt to be realistic—since confirmed by the phenomenon of enormous economic activity and expansion throughout the century. The acceleration of commerce and industry and growing prosperity seemed evidence enough of the wisdom of Enlightenment ideals; extend reason and science through the social body and all will be well. In much of American academic literature and in public addresses the glories of science were recounted and extolled. "Science" generally denoted practical, innovative, labor-saving devices and industrial techniques.

This Enlightenment Reason was not Kant's Pure Reason uncontaminated by acquisitive desires and earthly facts: it was Practical Reason, as Fichte had argued and romantic idealists urged further in critically revising Kantian doctrine: it was scientific and imaginative and instrumental, alive and in the world and the spirit of growth. Regarding the scene in 1818, Jefferson wrote: "When I contemplate the immense advances in science and the arts which have been made within the period of my life, I look forward with confidence to equal advances by the present generation, and I have no doubt they will consequently be as much wiser than we have been as we than our fathers were, and they than the burners of witches."[6]

One might wonder how the celebration of science and industry as instruments of progress accorded with the Puritan temper and the older established religious sentiments and convictions. In two very different ways reconciliation of a sort was effected, ways so contrasting as to add to the variety and increasing diversity of American moral experience. One way, espoused by President John Quincy Adams, and expounded by philosophical theologians such as McCosh of Princeton, was to affirm that, as Adams put it, "progressive improvement in the condition of man is apparently the purpose of a superintending Providence."[7] This is to say God's plan was evolutionary: the apparently secular manifestations of progress and prosperity were due to His dispensation. The other quite different religious and moral response to the great secular prosperity in American life was to draw a definite line between the weekday work of the body and the weekend resources of the spirit. The ethos of business and the ideal of "making good"—a peculiarly American idiom—prevailed for five- or six-sevenths of the seven-day week. The Sabbath was kept on the seventh day.

Thus two incompatible ethical conceptions of man's condition and prospects of this world, and his relation to his fellow men, were forced to inhabit the same house of clay and to dwell uneasily together. There was always friction and an acute sense of divided loyalties to two different masters; a dilemma that persistently and effectively provoked American philosophers to seek for some solution in a unification—if need be, even in a future spiritual community of ethical ideals and social reality. Emerson and Thoreau had sharply criticized this deep division in popular moral sentiment between what was regarded as good and right, and the devotions of might, King Cotton, the almighty dollar, gold in the bank.

So into the nineteenth-century paradise, as in all interesting paradises, there comes a serpent. The serpent is discord. There are occasions when growth and progress will serve almost as synonyms; but it does not require much effort of discernment to discover cases of growth that are not progress. American history is such a record of periodic disruption and mounting discord that one wonders how the notion of inevitable progress rooted itself so powerfully in the mind of laymen and visionaries. But history thrives on trickery, as Hegel observed; and while history is not myth, myths can become factors in the making of history. In America the population accelerated, cities grew, the laboring force grew, captains of industry sprouted, great fortunes were made. Growth there certainly was, but universal progress was less clearly manifested. Union had been won in the War of Independence, and almost lost in the War of 1812 when the North, fearing the effects upon commerce, opposed the expansionist proponents of war from the agricultural South and West. But the great conflict and threat of disunion came mid-century with the Civil War. That clash had been looming since the Missouri Compromise of 1820. Jefferson described the controversy then as "like a fire bell in the night," it "awakened and filled me with terror. I considered it at once as the knell of the Union."[8]

The debate over principles between spokesmen from the South and North as both sides moved toward war is highly instructive. Both Lincoln and Jefferson Davis derived their quite different cases from roughly the same premises of individual rights stated in the Constitution. It was the interpretation of rights and their consequences that differed. The question of a right of secession had arisen earlier; South Carolina had threatened to secede in 1833 in nullifying the Tariff Acts of 1828 and 1832, only to incur the wrath and insistence of the primacy of the Union from that hero of the South and West, President Andrew Jackson. And the North, led by President John Quincy Adams, had issued a similar threat in 1843.

The main issue of controversy before and during the war was whether or not the institution of slavery was a right granted in the Constitution. Southerners argued that it was; and the various compromises from 1820 onward between the North and South on the rights of slaveowners seemed to support the Southern position. Daniel Webster of the North saw no solution of the question in the Constitution. In response to the view that slavery was a constitutional right, William Lloyd Garrison burned a copy of the Constitution in a meeting in Boston in 1854. Nine years earlier, he had almost been lynched by a Boston crowd for his radical abolitionist opinions.

The Dred Scott decision of 1857 held that slavery could not be excluded from the territories of the Northwest. A slave was property and the Constitution guaranteed the rights of property. This was a victory for the South. The judgment declares itself to be based on "the words of the Constitution," rather than heeding subsequent changes in public opinion. The decision was an exercise in the explication of meaning; it claimed to speak for, or translate, the Constitution "not only in the same words but with the same meaning and intent with which it spoke when it came from the hands of its framers." There is a question, however, as Lincoln pointed out in his debates with Douglas, of the plausibility of the interpretation. And there is a broader question of the proper method of interpretation of the Constitution generally. This is a problem for constitutional lawyers and, interestingly, three of the members of the Metaphysical Club in Cambridge were lawyers. But the student of philosophy can profit by a study of the techniques employed. All the traditional theories of meaning are exhibited in the controversies: appeals are made to motives and to ideas in the minds of the founders, to the intuitions and inspirations reflected in the words. It should be noticed that all sides to the stormy conflict accepted the Constitution. This was a common ground: the quarrel was over the meaning. The debates over construction shared the common assumption that somewhere within the thicket of words there were essences or unalloyed nuggets of fixed meanings. For the Cambridge pragmatists, notably Oliver Wendell Holmes in this connection, the method of analysis and interpretation was not a retrospective search of original essences, but a prospective study of the consequences of language issuing in specifiable and predictable forms of social behavior.

A very different source of controversy, but concurrent with and like the slavery question also raising difficulties of constitutional interpretation and the relationship of federal and state powers, concerned financial policy and activities. Questions of money, so dear to us all, have roots in the subsoil of philosophy, so native to us all. The Civil War and its aftermath stimulated a wide variety of theories concerning how and to what extent the role of the federal government should be in the control and support of paper money and credit. With the rapid expansion of industry, agriculture, and the railroads westward, business transacted by notes and credit was a practical necessity; but the unstable relation of paper money to gold, manipulations and fluctuations of interest, were recurrent problems.

In the Middle West farming belt, once a land of plenty, overproduction accompanied by depression, indebtedness, and increasing rates on produce and railway transportation encouraged a Jacksonian rebellion against Eastern banks and producers who controlled the money. In the East, also inspired by Jacksonian ideals of free enterprise, the aim rather was as far as possible to manage by private groups the constitutional right to "coin money and regulate the value thereof." Interesting and diverse theories of money and value emerged from the discussions and political meetings. English theorists and Parliament had set certain guidelines concerning gold as the standard value for paper money and notes. Hence, the prevailing tendency was to think of gold as constituting real value (comparable to fixed essences for meaning) while paper money was a useful convention (comparable to signs and words, the legal tender of meaning). William James changed this figure slightly but echoed some of these controversies in speaking of pragmatism as giving the "cash value" of abstract concepts and describing the system of truths as a "credit system" in which our "beliefs 'pass'...just as bank-notes pass" so long as they are not refused. But the system of beliefs requires direct verifications somewhere or it will collapse "like a financial system with no cash basis."[9] The simile has a history going back into earlier centuries of mercantilist theory.

It was generally agreed that the Civil War had been chaotically and wastefully financed. The National Bank Act of 1863 attempted to introduce order by retiring greenbacks and reducing the government's role in credit by refunding debts in gold and making paper money redeemable for gold. The result was a severe deflation and diminishing of the circulation of money. As the farmer watched perplexed, his newborn calf grew in size while shrinking in value. He would join the Greenback Party of 1876 which advocated expanding the currency by circulation of greenbacks. Questions were raised concerning gold as an absolute value, even to proposing that it was an exchangeable value or commodity convertible into other goods. One writer proposed a system of banknotes fixed by the productive wealth of the country; the latter is "real value." He criticized what he regarded as the "aristocratic" gold theorists for maintaining "such words as *safe, secured, national, uniform, economical, inalienable,* when predicated of anything but gold as currency, are...mere sounds devoid of significance."[10] The criticism is clear; gold is not the only object of which these predications are true—controlled credit will do as well. The dispute has some resemblance to those once held over the doctrine of transubstantiation: can wholly different substances (or subjects) share the same properties (or predicates)? In any case, the technical question is one of criteria of meaningful predicates and predication; and the general social question was to determine whose interests were best served by the control of money and credit. The populists and democratic theorists had one answer, the bankers and industrialists had another.

I come to a final illustration of the period of confusion, aggressive growth and expansion after the war that were factors in the wider historical background in which the Metaphysical Club and pragmatism had their origins.

An outstanding feature of social life in the cities during the last quarter of the nineteenth century was the crude forms of pecuniary aggression and extraordinary civic corruption. While the Metaphysical Club was meeting in Cambridge, the Tammany Club of Boss Tweed was holding meetings in New York. From 1869 to 1871 that group controlled New York politics and a major part of its finances. By 1871 the ring had accomplished the theft of $20,000,000. The shining symbol of this achievement was Tweed's courthouse: planned to cost not more than $250,000, more than $8,000,000 were siphoned into its expenditures, and it was never completed. New York was also the scene of the famous Erie War between Fiske, Drew, and Gould and Commodore Vanderbilt over control of the railroad. Each side bought public officials and paid Senators in Albany for their votes. Speaking of the Erie War but reflecting on the conditions of the cities generally, Henry Adams wrote: "The worst scandals of the eighteenth century were relatively harmless by the side of this, which smirched executive, judiciary, banks, corporate systems, professions, and people, all the great active forces of society, in one dirty cesspool of vulgar corruption."[11]

But it was not only in New York that corruption flourished. In 1871, the City Treasurer of Philadelphia was discovered to have defrauded the Home of Independence and Brotherly Love of $478,000. The Chicago fire seems to have dispelled its leading ring of plunderers and destroyed the incriminating records. In 1868 the *Nation* commented: "There is hardly a legislature in the country which is not suspected of corruption; there is hardly a court over which some suspicion does not hang."[12] One year after this editorial appeared, that extraordinary trio of predatory finance—Gould, Drew, and Fiske—attempted to corner the gold supply of the nation and succeeded in bringing about the great banking crisis of the day.

II.

The foregoing are but samples of problems generated from deeper conditions of conflict and variance in American life in the latter half of the nineteenth century. It is especially to be noticed that the problems are matched in their seriousness and urgency by their complexity. Difficult theoretical and conceptual issues are inseparable from others possessing enormous practical significance and wide-ranging social consequences.

These conditions of intellectual uncertainty and predicament in competing norms and demands of conduct are among the formative dispositions and historical origins of pragmatism. They are not, of course, the academic sources of doctrine, that inheritance of European thought and distillations made of it in Cambridge which we touched on earlier. It is the combining and amalgamation of academic doctrine with novel and changing social institutions that shaped the general history of pragmatism and its more distinctive features.

One social institution subject to elusive forms of inflation and debasement in times of great stress is language. It is an old story. Thucydides commented on the effects of crisis and revolution in the Greek cities in 427 B.C.: "The ordinary value of words in relation to things was changed as was thought fitting. Irrational audacity came to be regarded as courage...cautious forethought as specious cowardice, moderation as a screen for unmanliness...the violent was always trusted, his opponent was viewed with suspicion."[13] He attributes all this and more to the lust for power originating from greed and ambition. One of the motives of Plato's theory of Forms was to establish a dispassionate and objective criterion of knowledge and the informed use of language and to expose, thereby, misuses of the medium. Sometime about 1670, a group of gentlemen were discussing vexing questions of morality and religion when one of them, John Locke, felt it necessary before arriving at a "resolution of these doubts," to engage in a prior clarification of language and the Understanding. Hence the great *Essay* of 1690. In the energetic and unstable post-Civil War period in America, in the club in Cambridge, another group of gentlemen were to recognize again the need for clarification and determination of the uses of language as essential to the solution of difficult problems. As in the past, the critique and reformation of thought and language proceeds according to some exemplar or idea of clarity and stability. Plato seems to have looked to medicine and mathematics in developing the theory of Forms; Locke looked to Newtonian science. The pragmatists looked to nineteenth-century science, notably the theory of evolution and statistical methods.

The intellectual atmosphere in Cambridge—in contrast to the prosperous, esthete, genteel tradition of Brahmin Boston—was enlightened, scientific, and agnostic. Thus Peirce remarked that "The Metaphysical Club" was intended as partly an ironical, partly a defiant title. Spencer was the dominant philosophic influence of the time although soon to be dispelled by a powerful advance of Anglo-Hegelian absolute idealism. In an influential essay of 1859, Spencer had advocated scientific education rather than the traditional curriculum of the classics as indispensable in the modern world.[14] Ten years later, President Eliot of Harvard introduced the elective system largely as a way of accommodating demands on higher education, permitting students to avoid the rigors of a cumbersome classical and humanistic program of studies and prepare more directly for roles in science, industry, and business. (The pressure for "relevant studies" was on even then.)

The paradigm, then, of conceptual clarity, of reliable judgment and of intellectual progress, was science. The doctrine of pragmatism that emerged from the Metaphysical Club, to be further developed by Peirce, James, and Dewey, was a profoundly suggestive attempt to apply and extend insights gleaned from the methods and strategy utilized in experimental science to philosophic subject matters. The shaping of the doctrine, initially a technique for achieving linguistic and conceptual clarity, led to the development of a critical theory of the function and relative uses of conceptual structures in the control of passing and future experience. The theory, as I see it, emerged as a general conception of practical reason and the purposive nature of thought; of knowledge as an instrument of action; and of the inseparable and primary connection of meaning and action. In the theory there is also a linking of value and knowledge—knowledge conceived as a form of action and the realization of value. C. I. Lewis put it succinctly: "Pragmatism might almost be defined as the contention that all judgments of truth are judgments of value; that verification is a value-determination; and the criterion of truth is realization of some kind of value."[15]

III.

I have been emphasizing disparity, disequilibrium, and patterns of violence in the wider nineteenth-century setting in which the Cambridge Club was situated as among the prehensile roots of the history of pragmatism. The pragmatists' interest in a method of making our ideas clear; of resolving disputed questions provoking philosophical analysis; of conceptual clarity as a condition of successful action, reflects an ideal of equilibrium and stability in intellectual affairs.

In all this, I do not want to be misunderstood. Mine is not a thesis of historical or sociological determinism. I do not intend to suggest that Peirce's maxim and the technical extensions of it were merely products of historical forces acting on the minds of the members of the Metaphysical Club. This would be to overlook the other formative academic origins of pragmatism acknowledged earlier and among these, especially, the intense and serious efforts and ensuing controversies over the interpretation and larger intellectual and moral implications of Darwinism that occupied the club and other Cambridge thinkers as well. My point is only that the special interest in an effective method for clarifying beliefs and the analysis of concepts in the club, circa 1872, was *partially* stimulated by powerful divisive and conflicting interests and activities occurring and evident on the historical scene in the late nineteenth century. And this is to suggest at most that the impulse then to develop a method of clarifying ideas, claims, and policies was generated from more than purely theoretical and academic philosophical considerations (important as these latter were). My more specific suggestion at the moment is that this same impulse reflected a concern to stabilize and purify language which, under the stress, was subject to debasement, confusion, and misuses in wider social contexts. This was an effort to introduce a moral as well as a methodological reform of language and thought: an affirmation of critical intelligence as not only indispensable to discerning and assessing possible goods, but also essential to a new view of experience as basically experimental in character. This impulse led Peirce and Dewey eventually to a vision of an increasingly rational and progressing community dedicated to the resolution of differences through the application of scientific inquiry; it led James somewhat differently to view pragmatism as a way of mediating claims and determining the legitimate scope and expression of preferences among individuals as of primary importance.

But while an understanding of the factors that generate thought may help us appreciate the subsequent developments, it does not disclose predestined conclusions. The pragmatists regarded thought as initiated by doubt, irritation, and hesitancy, and culminating—if at all—in the satisfaction of belief. I should not wish here to depart so widely from that conception as to suggest that the historical occasion of intellectual itch is all there is to theoretical scratch.

In any case, we have moved some distance from the charge that pragmatism is a defense of American big business. And this final note brings us back to Peirce's view of scientific thought as thoroughly social in impulse and outcome.

Within the social function of thought and language originates the idea of external reality so important, as we earlier noticed Peirce arguing, to our understanding of science and the truth of belief. For our sense of externally real things comes through language as we first acquire it. Externality is coercive over our sensibility; and one such coercive pressure is the very process of trial and correction in which we gradually learn to use language, beginning with the most object-directed segments of speech. Critical pragmatism is the systematic effort of reduction and translation of unclear language to clearer and more reliable uses—facilitating, as it goes, our capacity to mean what we say and say what we mean. It also enjoins us to heed the responsibilities we assume in sharing a language in common for its preservation in the future: responsibilities of conceptualization and conduct as agencies of control over external conditions directed to the realization of significance and value for the common good. In this task pragmatism is a kind of metaphilosophy—not a system, but, as James pictures it, more like a corridor leading out into various systems and theorizing. Still, central to the corridor and running its course are the critical lines of interest in meaning and truth, the life-lines, so to speak, of coherence and communication.

H. S. Thayer

Even in the technical principle of pragmatism, as enunciated by Peirce and James, we can witness the social role conceived for it within the public body of beliefs and conduct. The analysis of an expression, its translation into a description of experimental operations, or actions and predictable effects, is a kind of organizing of some central group of statements so as to clarify one troublesome case. There is also the fitting of this information into the larger established body of statements, our system of beliefs. James thought of this aspect of the procedure as one defining condition of truth: the integrating of new beliefs into the older stock of knowledge. And we might notice that this integrative procedure extends in principle, by implication, through the body, from scientific statements, so-called, to moral and aesthetic convictions, and back again.

Thus, to clarify meaning is not in any one case an isolated procedure—as perhaps theorists of constitutional construction, for example, have assumed it to be. The clarification affects, and is affected by, the truths of statements throughout the system. We have learned to be suspicious of the notion of meaning as captured essences. We can also question the notion of meanings as captured in single expressions. The visual or auditory representation of isolated groups of inscriptions, printed or uttered, can mislead us to supposing that meanings reside within the graphic borders or sounds, as atoms of thought. But if we study the maxim urged by Peirce, James, and Dewey, we see that specification of meaning is an elaborate, socially conditioned maneuver in which sentences are organized about some questionable fragment. The whole is brought to bear upon some difficult part. This is not, however, only or merely assimilation, because the reconstruction of meaning is sensitive to effects and consequences in ongoing experience and to the interests as well of the community participating in and utilizing the common language. So far, we have basic agreement among Peirce, James, and Dewey, and reaching—despite other differences—to Lewis and Quine.

The pragmatic conception of knowledge and value as modes of action subject to testable terminations in experience and guided by predictable properties of the physical world is, as Lewis said, a "flight from subjectivity." For the stress is upon the real world as at once an object of knowledge as well as the means of its vital operations; a world encountered, shared, enjoyed, and communicated in common.

NOTES

1. For the text of this address, *see* Appendix I in *Pragmatism, The Works of William James* (Cambridge, Mass.: Harvard University Press, 1975).
2. *Pragmatism*, p. 29.
3. Charles Sanders Peirce, *Collected Papers* (Cambridge, Mass.: Harvard University Press, 1931-1958), 5:358-87.
4. *Pragmatism*, p. 28.
5. Peirce, *Collected Papers*, 7:267.
6. Letter to Dr. Waterhouse, March 3, 1818. Adrienne Koch and William Peden, eds., *The Life and Selected Writings of Thomas Jefferson* (New York: The Modern Library, 1944), p. 687.
7. Fourth of July Address, Quincy, Mass., 1821. *See* A.A. Ekirch, *The Idea of Progress in America* (New York: Columbia University Press, 1944), p. 73.
8. Letter to John Holmes, April 22, 1980. *Life and Selected Writings*, p. 69.
9. *Pragmatism*, p. 100.
10. Eleazar Lord, *National Currency: A Review of the National Banking Law*, 1863. Quoted in Vernon L. Parrington, *Main Currents in American Thought* (New York: Harcourt, Brace and Company, 1930), III, 274.
11. *The Education of Henry Adams* (Boston and New York: Houghton Mifflin Company, 1918), pp. 271-72.
12. *The Nation*, 6(May 14, 1868), quoted in Allen Nevins, *The Emergence of America 1865-1878* (New York: Macmillan Co., 1927), p. 180. Our sorry Watergate era had precedents. In 1856 Walt Whitman viewed the scene thus: "...every trustee of the people is a traitor, looking only to his own gain, and to boost up his party. The berths, the Presidency included, are bought, sold, electioneered for, prostituted, and filled with prostitutes." "The Eighteenth Presidency!" *Complete Poetry & Selected Prose and Letters* (London: The Nonesuch Press, n.d.), p. 588.
13. Thucydides, III, 82.
14. "What Knowledge Is of Most Worth?" *Westminster and Foreign Quarterly Review*, 31(July 1859), 1-41. Reprinted in *Education* (New York: Appleton and Company, 1860). Spencer's answer to the question in his title is: Science. He concluded: "Science proclaimed as highest alike in worth and beauty, will reign supreme." On the other side it was Matthew Arnold who

was probably the most influential advocate of humanistic classics in education. *See* Merle Curti, *The Growth of American Thought* (New York: Harper & Brothers, 1943), p. 87; and for the background in education, V.T. Thayer, *Formative Ideas in American Education* (New York: Dodd, Mead & Company, 1965), p. 172.

15. John D. Goheen and John L. Mothershead, Jr., eds. *Collected Papers of Clarence Irving Lewis* (Stanford, Calif.: Stanford University Press, 1970), p. 280. Lewis also wrote, "Pragmatism...could be characterized as the doctrine that all problems are at bottom problems of conduct, that all judgments are, implicitly, judgments of value, and that, as there can be ultimately no valid distinction of theoretical from practical, so there can be no final separation of questions of truth of any kind from questions of the justifiable ends of action." Ibid., p. 108.

THE PRAGMATISTS' PLACE IN EMPIRICISM

W. V. QUINE

IT IS NOT CLEAR TO ME what it takes to be a pragmatist. It is not clear in what ways the philosophers who have been called pragmatists are nearer in outlook to one another than to philosophers who are not so called. I suspect that the term 'pragmatism' is one we could do without. It draws a pragmatic blank. However, we have the term, and we can make some sense of it by enumeration. Peirce, James, Schiller, Mead, and Dewey have been called pragmatists and have owned the soft impeachment.

All of these professing or card-carrying pragmatists belong, it seems, to the empiricist tradition. I shall begin by scanning that tradition. In the past two centuries there have been, I think, five points where empiricism has taken a turn for the better. I propose to describe these five turning points and then examine various of our professing pragmatists with respect to them. If anything indicative comes out, it could suggest to what extent pragmatism abetted the progress of empiricism. It could also suggest to what extent pragmatism was on the right track, even if only as follower rather than leader. And finally it could suggest to what extent I am a pragmatist. This third objective is more interesting to me than to many. Still, on reflection, it doesn't really differ from the second. After all, when I judge whether pragmatism is on the right track, I am judging whether it is on my track; for naturally I take the track that is right by my lights.

I shall ignore a prominent range of topics in the writings of the pragmatists, namely, those having to do with the theory of values. For I am concerned here to relate myself to pragmatism, and I have not myself dealt with the theory of values.

The first of the five turning points of empiricism that I have in mind is the shift from ideas to words. The second is the shift of semantic focus from terms to sentences. The third is the shift of semantic focus from sentences to systems of sentences. The fourth is, in White's phrase, methodological monism: abandonment of the analytic-synthetic dualism. The fifth is naturalism: abandonment of the goal of a first philosophy prior to science. I shall proceed to elaborate on each of the five.

The first was the shift of center from ideas to words. This was the adoption of the policy, in epistemology, of talking about linguistic expressions where possible instead of ideas. This policy was of course pursued by the medieval nominalists, but I think of it as entering modern empiricism only in 1786. Writing in that year, John Horne Tooke maintained that if we were to substitute the word 'word' everywhere that Locke wrote the word 'idea,' Locke's essay would be the better.

British empiricism was dedicated to the proposition that only sense makes sense. Ideas were acceptable only if based on sense impressions. But Tooke appreciated that the idea itself measures up poorly to empiricist standards. Translated into Tooke's terms, the basic proposition of British empiricism would seem to say that words make sense only insofar as they are definable in sensory terms.

At this point, trouble arises over grammatical particles: what of our prepositions, our conjunctions, our copula? These are indispensable to coherent discourse, yet how are they definable in sensory terms? John Horne Tooke adopted a heroic line here, arguing that the particles were really ordinary concrete terms in degenerate form. He advanced ingenious etymologies: 'if' was 'give,' 'but' was 'be out.' However, this line was needless and hopeless. If we could make concrete terms do all the work of the grammatical particles, we could make them do so without awaiting justification from the side of etymology. But surely we cannot, and there is no valid reason to want to; for there is another approach to the problem of defining the grammatical particles in sensory terms. We have only to recognize that they are *syncategorematic*. They are definable not in isolation but in context.

This brings us to the second of the five turning points, the shift from terms to sentences. The medievals had the notion of syncategorematic words, but it was a contemporary of John Horne Tooke, namely, Jeremy Bentham, who developed it into an explicit theory of contextual definition. He applied contextual definition not just to grammatical particles and the like, but even to some genuine terms, categorematic ones. If he found some term convenient but ontologically embarrassing, contextual definition enabled him in some cases to continue to enjoy the services of the term while disclaiming its denotation. He could declare the term syncategorematic, despite grammatical appearances, and then could justify his continued use of it if he could show systematically how to paraphrase as wholes all sentences in which he chose to imbed it. Such was his theory of fictions:[1] what he called paraphrasis, and what we now call contextual definition. The term, like the grammatical particles, is meaningful as a part of meaning. If every sentence in which we use a term can be paraphrased into a sentence that makes good sense, no more can be asked.

Comfort could be derived from Bentham's doctrine of paraphrasis by all who may have inherited Locke's and Hume's misgivings over abstract ideas. Reconsidered in the spirit of John Horne Tooke, these misgivings became misgivings over abstract terms; and then Bentham's approach offers hope of accommodating such terms, in some contexts anyway, without conceding an ontology of abstract objects. I am persuaded that one cannot thus make a clean sweep of all abstract objects without sacrificing much of science, including classical mathematics. But certainly one can pursue those nominalistic aims much further than could have been clearly conceived in the days before Bentham and Tooke.

Contextual definition precipitated a revolution in semantics: less sudden perhaps than the Copernican revolution in astronomy, but like it in being a shift of center. The primary vehicle of meaning is seen no longer as the word, but as the sentence. Terms, like grammatical particles, mean by contributing to the meaning of the sentences that contain them. The heliocentrism propounded by Copernicus was not obvious, and neither is this. It is not obvious because, for the most part, we understand sentences only by construction from understood words. This is necessarily so, since sentences are potentially infinite in variety. We learn some words in isolation, in effect as one-word sentences; we learn further words in context, by learning various short sentences that contain them; and we understand further sentences by construction from the words thus learned. If the language that we thus learn is afterward compiled, the manual will necessarily consist for the most part of a word-by-word dictionary, thus obscuring the fact that the meanings of words are abstractions from the truth conditions of sentences that contain them.

It was the recognition of this semantic primacy of sentences that gave us contextual definition, and vice versa. I attributed this to Bentham. Generations later we find Frege celebrating the semantic primacy of sentences, and Russell giving contextual definition its fullest exploitation in technical logic. But Bentham's contribution had not been lying ineffective all that while. In the course of the nineteenth century a practice emerged in the differential calculus of using differential operators in such a way as to simulate coefficients, while recognizing that the operators were really intelligible only as fragments of larger terms. It was this usage, indeed, rather than Bentham's writings, that directly inspired Russell's contextual definitions.[2]

In consequence of the shift of attention from term to sentence, epistemology came in the twentieth century to be a critique not primarily of concepts but of truths and beliefs. The verification theory of meaning, which dominated the Vienna Circle, was concerned with the meaning and meaningfulness of sentences rather than of words. The English philosophers of ordinary language have likewise directed their analyses to sentences rather than to words, in keeping with the example that was set by both the earlier and the later work of their mentor Wittgenstein. Bentham's lesson penetrated and permeated epistemology in the fullness of time.

The next move, number three in my five, shifts the focus from sentences to systems of sentences. We come to recognize that in a scientific theory even a whole sentence is ordinarily too short a text to serve as an independent vehicle of empirical meaning. It will not have its separable bundle of observable or testable consequences. A reasonably inclusive body of scientific theory, taken as a whole, will indeed have such consequences. The theory will imply a lot of observation conditionals, as I call them, each of which says that if certain observable conditions are met, then a certain observable event will occur. But, as Duhem has emphasized, these observation conditionals are implied only by the theory as a whole. If any of them proves false, then the theory is false, but on the face of it there is no saying which of the component sentences of the theory is to blame. The observation conditionals cannot be distributed as consequences of the several sentences of the theory. Typically, no one sentence of the theory implies any of the observation conditionals.

The scientist does indeed test a single sentence of his theory by observation conditionals, but only through having chosen to treat that sentence as vulnerable and the rest, for the time being, as firm. This is the situation when he is testing a new hypothesis with a view to adding it, if he may, to his growing system of beliefs.

When we look thus to a whole theory or system of sentences as the vehicle of empirical meaning, how inclusive should we take this system to be? Should it be the whole of science—or the whole of *a* science, a branch of science? This should be seen as a matter of degree, and of diminishing returns. All sciences interlock to some extent; they share a common logic and generally some common part of mathematics, even when nothing else. It is an uninteresting legalism, however, to think of our scientific system of the world as involved *en bloc* in every prediction. More modest chunks suffice, and so may be ascribed their independent empirical meaning, nearly enough, since some vagueness in meaning must be allowed for in any event.

It would also be wrong to suppose that *no* single sentence of a theory has its separable empirical meaning. Theoretical sentences grade off to observation sentences; observationality is a matter of degree, namely, the degree of spontaneous agreement that the sentence would command from present witnesses. And while it may be argued that even an observation sentence may be recanted in the light of the rest of one's theory, this is an extreme case and happily not characteristic. And in any event there will be single sentences at the other extreme—long theoretical ones—that surely have their separable empirical meaning, for we can make a conjunctive sentence of a whole theory.

Thus the holism that the third move brings should be seen only as a moderate or relative holism. What is important is that we cease to demand or expect of a scientific sentence that it have its own separable empirical meaning.

The fourth move, to methodological monism, follows closely on this holism. Holism blurs the supposed contrast between the synthetic sentence, with its empirical content, and the analytic sentence with its null content. The organizing role that was supposedly the role of analytic sentences is now seen shared by sentences generally, and the empirical content that was supposedly peculiar to synthetic sentences is now seen as diffused through the system.

The fifth move, finally, brings naturalism: abandonment of the goal of a first philosophy. It sees natural science as an inquiry into reality, fallible and corrigible but not answerable to any supra-scientific tribunal, and not in need of any justification beyond observation and the hypothetico-deductive method. Naturalism has two sources, both negative. One of them is despair of being able to define theoretical terms generally in terms of phenomena, even by contextual definition. A holistic or system-centered attitude should suffice to produce this despair. The other negative source of naturalism is unregenerate realism, the robust state of mind of the natural scientist who has never felt any qualms beyond the negotiable uncertainties internal to science. Naturalism had a representative already in 1830 in the antimetaphysician Auguste Comte, who declared that "positive philosophy" does not differ in method from the special sciences.

Naturalism does not repudiate epistemology, but assimilates it to empirical psychology. Science itself tells us that our information about the world is limited to irritations to our surfaces, and then the epistemological question is in turn a question within science: the question how we human animals can have managed to arrive at science from such limited information. Our scientific epistemologist pursues this inquiry and comes out with an account that has a good deal to do with the learning of language and with the neurology of perception. He talks of how men posit bodies and hypothetical particles, but he does not mean to suggest that the things thus posited do not exist. Evolution and natural selection will doubtless figure in this account, and he will feel free to apply physics if he sees a way.

The naturalistic philosopher begins his reasoning within the inherited world theory as a going concern. He tentatively believes all of it, but believes also that some unidentified portions are wrong. He tries to improve, clarify, and understand the system from within. He is the busy sailor adrift on Neurath's boat.

Pragmatists' Place in Empiricism

These, then, are what I think of as the five significant advances in post-Humean empiricism. They form the background against which I want now to view the professing pragmatists, beginning with Peirce. His celebrated "pragmatic maxim" of 1878 ran thus: "Consider what effects, that might conceivably have practical bearings, we conceive the object of our conception to have. Then, our conception of these effects is the whole of our conception of the object."[3] In this passage we see no effect of John Horne Tooke's shift from ideas to words, let alone Bentham's shift from words to sentences. Peirce's eye, like Hume's, is evidently on the idea: the conception.

Actually Peirce's attitude was more Benthamite, more sentence-centered, than this ill-phrased passage suggests. In Peirce a dominant role accrues to sentences through his preoccupation with belief; for the primary objects of belief are perforce sentences, or, at worst, propositions. Peirce's behavioral account of belief, in terms of dispositions to action, even promises a behavioral account of sentence meanings likewise in terms of dispositions to action; for the meaning of a sentence could be explained as comprising those very dispositions to action that constitute belief in the truth of the sentence. Thus the meaning of the sentence *is* the belief. Odd verbally, but why not?

The phrase "practical bearings" in the pragmatic maxim fits nicely with Peirce's account of belief as disposition to action. This interpretation is corroborated in the following passage: "...the most perfect account of a concept that words can convey will consist in a description of the habit which that concept is calculated to produce. But how otherwise can a habit be described than by a description of the kind of action to which it gives rise...?"[4] Interpreted along this line, the pragmatic maxim amounts to saying that our conception of an object is the aggregate of our beliefs about the object, in Peirce's behavioral sense of belief. Putting this in a more explicitly semantic form, we might say that the meaning of a term for a man is the aggregate of all the sentences that contain the term and are believed by the man. This succession of transformations thus ends in depicting Peirce's pragmatic maxim itself as really oriented to sentences after all, despite the perversity of his phrasing. Sentence meaning stands forth as basic, and term meaning falls into place as derivative.

This reading of Peirce's pragmatic maxim accords well with some passages, but must be supplemented by an alternative reading to accommodate such passages as this: "...If one can define accurately all the conceivable experimental phenomena which the affirmation or denial of a concept could imply, one will have therein a complete definition of the concept...."[5] The orientation to sentences is gratifyingly explicit here in the words 'affirmation or denial,' despite retention of the word 'concept.' Habits of action, however, cease to figure here; it is a question now of "experimental phenomena." To accommodate this passage, we must read the phrase "have practical bearings," in the pragmatic maxim simply as "be observable." Rephrased as a criterion of the meaning of sentences, the idea is simply that the meaning of a sentence consists in the difference that its truth or falsity would make to possible experience. Meaning is empirical meaning; the meaning of a sentence consists in its observable consequences. It is the verification theory of meaning, echoed in the Vienna Circle. I find difficulty in regarding it as distinctive of pragmatism. Any empiricist, if asked about the meaning of sentences, might have been expected to come out with something like this.

It will be well to compare Mach with Peirce on a few points. They were close contemporaries; Mach was a year and a half older. He came to be the inspiration and acknowledged precursor of the Vienna Circle. But Bentham's shift of focus from term to sentence, which was to be so fully accepted in the Vienna Circle, seems to have missed Mach. He was oriented still to terms and their objects rather than to sentences and their truth conditions.

Peirce's pragmatic maxim likewise was phrased in the pre-Benthamite way, we saw; but his preoccupation with belief shows him to have been oriented somewhat more to sentences than Mach was. Mach's empiricist scruples were directed upon terms, whose business was denotation; and the terms compatible with his empiricist scruples were terms for sensation. His was an ontology of sensations, rather in the spirit of Hume's. On the other hand, Peirce explicitly repudiated the sensationalist ontology, in favor of an ontology dominated largely by dispositions,[6] whose linguistic kin are sentences: conditional sentences. In the hardness test, what was real for Mach was the sight of the scratch; what was real for Peirce was the disposition to scratch.

Despite its ready appeal, despite its acceptance by both Peirce and the Vienna Circle, the verification theory of sentence meanings is not one to rest with. We must hold out for a holistic or system-centered semantics. Now Peirce was unquestionably aware that scientific theory confronts its evidence thus holistically. You who read Peirce more patiently than I can doubtless cite many passages to this effect. But such awareness is hard to reconcile with his facile account of pragmatic meaning, or of one's conception of an object.[7]

When he moves on to his theory of truth, he does treat scientific theory more holistically. Truth is the limit approached by theory under persistent use of scientific method, and he is at pains to explain at length what counts as scientific method. But the limit theory is untenable. It depends on a notion of successive approximation on the part of theories, and this supposes that we know what it means to compare theories in respect to degree of similarity. No such criterion of similarity is offered. And this is not the worst of it. There is not only a problem of comparing the degrees of similarity of theories; there is also a problem even of comparing theories for identity and difference at all. This is a problem of translation: a question whether to equate the words from theory to theory, even when the words are literally the same. If we are merely comparing two little theories that are rival candidates for filling some limited corner of our comprehensive system of the world, then this latter problem of identity and difference is not so serious, for we adhere to the language of our comprehensive system across the board. But where it is a question of rival systems of the world, we have no fixed frame to cleave to. A third criticism, justly leveled by Ayer, is that "...an enormous number of propositions, which we shall wish to characterize as true or false, will not be able either to pass or to fail the test, simply because their candidature will have lapsed. For it can hardly be supposed that even in the scientific millennium a complete historical record will have been kept of every particular event."[8]

This limit theory of truth is distinctive of Peirce and perhaps, therefore, of pragmatism, but the word 'pragmatism' in no way suggests it. At points, moreover, we find Peirce slipping into quite another theory of truth, better suited to the word 'pragmatism.' Thus he writes that the test of the hypothesis of the existence of God "must lie in the self-controlled growth of man's conduct of life."[9] Also he remarked on the anthropocentric bias of his philosophy.[10] His admirer, F.C.S. Schiller, even adopted the name 'humanism' for his own brand of purported pragmatism. Perhaps Peirce's limit theory of truth should itself be construed anthropocentrically as a sort of idealism or social Protagoreanism, representing scientific method as dictating to reality.

Peirce does not lend himself readily to single-minded interpretation. We had to interpret his pragmatic maxim sometimes in terms of dispositions to actions and sometimes in terms of confirmatory experiences. William James made a loyal effort to accept the maxim in both interpretations. He wrote as follows:

> The ultimate test for us of what a truth means is indeed the conduct it dictates or inspires. But it inspires that conduct because it first foretells some particular turn to our experience which shall call for just that conduct from us. And I should prefer to express Peirce's principle by saying that the effective meaning of any philosophic proposition can always be brought down to some particular consequence, in our future practical experience, whether active or passive.[11]

The conduct inspired is the ultimate test, and the predictions are what inspire it. Why not just settle for the predictions and say, like any empiricist, that the test of a truth *is* the experience it foretells? What substance is added by calling the conduct the "ultimate" test? James was too loyal to Peirce's faltering line.

James's reference to conduct as the ultimate test recalls the passage that I quoted from Peirce on the existence of God: that the test "must lie in the self-controlled growth of man's conduct of life." Here is the precedent for James's notorious defense of wishful thinking. But how could James reconcile wishful thinking with the empiricist principle that truth is confirmed by predicted experience? He might argue that comfort is an experience, and comfort is a predictable consequence of belief in God, and the predicted comfort is indeed forthcoming, thus confirming the belief. To argue thus would be to confuse belief in God with existence of God. This seems

Pragmatists' Place in Empiricism

an unlikely confusion, but James seems in the end to have confessed to it. Morris and Perry quote a letter of 1907 in which James wrote to Lovejoy that he, James, had confused "consequences of true ideas *per se*, and consequences of ideas *qua believed by us*."[12]

James's kind words to wishful thinkers reverberated, though, as kind words will. They inspired F.C.S. Schiller. Schiller, with his philosophy of humanism, was Protagoras *redivivus*. But at this point, a funny thing happened. He had a doctrine of "postulation," which had us believing whatever we wish were true until it proves troublesome.[13] Now the funny thing is that this is a fair account of the hypothetico-deductive method—wishful thinking subject to correction. Apart from an indefinable element of fun, this is pretty much what Popper has described as conjecture and refutation. And incidentally, recalling my five steps of post-Humean empiricism, we may note that this postulational or hypothetico-deductive account is already well suited to the holistic or system-centered position.

Popper and the rest of us who celebrate the hypothetico-deductive method, depart from Schiller's humanism, it may be supposed, in thinking of it as a method of finding truth rather than making it. But I cannot agree. Despite my naturalism, I am bound to recognize that the systematic structure of scientific theory is man-made. It is made to fit the data, yes, but invented rather than discovered, because it is not uniquely determined by the data. Alternative systems, all undreamed of, would have fitted the data, too.

The pragmatists James, Schiller, and Dewey viewed science as a conceptual shorthand for organizing observations. Idealists in Europe held the same view: Mach, Pearson, Poincaré, perhaps Ramsey. And now I, for all my vaunted naturalism, seem drawn into the same position. Is there no difference?

The difference is to be sought in ontology. For James and the European idealists that I named, reality consisted primarily in sensation. Schiller's reality was a primordially formless substance shaped by the mind of man.[14] Dewey's reality consisted of observable objects.[15] Similarly, it seems, for Mead.[16] For naturalistic philosophers such as I, on the other hand, physical objects are real, right down to the most hypothetical of particles, though this recognition of them is subject, like all science, to correction. I can hold this ontological line of naive and unregenerate realism, and at the same time I can hail man as largely the author rather than discoverer of truth. I can hold both lines because the scientific truth about physical objects is still the *truth*, for all man's authorship. In my naturalism, I recognize no higher truth than that which science provides or seeks. The scientist is indeed creative, he posits the physical objects, and could perhaps have produced a different system that would fit all past and future data just as well; but to say all this is to affirm truths still within science, about science. These truths illuminate the methodology of our science but do not falsify or supersede our science. We make do with what we have and improve it when we see how. We are always talking within our going system when we attribute truth; we cannot talk otherwise. Our system changes, yes. When it does, we do not say that truth changes with it; we say that we had wrongly supposed something true and have learned better. Fallibilism is the watchword, not relativism. Fallibilism and naturalism.

These reflections on truth and ontology have not revealed any distinctive tenet of the pragmatists. James shared the sensationalist ontology of the idealists, we saw, but Peirce repudiated it, as I do. Dewey took an intermediate position, we saw, and Schiller another. Perhaps they all went along with the idealists, as I do, in regarding truth as human handwork at least to a high degree.

C. I. Lewis regarded himself as a sort of pragmatist, a *conceptual* pragmatist, because of holding a doctrine of man-made truth. His, however, was no sweeping idealism. Man-made truth on his view comprised much less than natural science; it comprised only what he called the *a priori*. He saw his doctrine as a pragmatic variant of Kant's. The categories had been immutable for Kant; immutable adjuncts of human nature. For Lewis they were pragmatic, they were matters of convenience, mutable by convention. They were a matter of how we chose to frame our concepts, or define our words. The man-made truths were analytic.

Lewis was thus in agreement with the Vienna Circle in rejecting Kant's synthetic *a priori*. But, like the Vienna Circle, Lewis stopped short of what I called the fourth step of post-Humean empiricism: abandonment of the analytic-synthetic dualism altogether.

Pragmatists' Place in Empiricism

I suggested earlier that the analytic-synthetic distinction may be expected to waver in a holistic or system-centered semantics. I would expect it to waver likewise in any far-reaching theory of man-made truth; one sentence would be as analytic as another. It is significant that Lewis, who set such store by the analytic-synthetic distinction, professed only a partial pragmatism, limiting it to the analytic truths. James rejected the distinction. Dewey was indecisive over it, according to White.[17]

What now of the fifth step of post-Humean empiricism, the move to naturalism? A few minutes ago, I dissociated myself from the idealists by flourishing my naturalist ontology; and in so doing, I left some of the professional pragmatists on the other side. Still James, despite his idealist ontology, and Dewey, despite his intermediate ontology, were decidedly naturalistic in their way of doing epistemology. Dewey claimed that "the whole of pragmatism in embryo" is James's doctrine that our important categories—space, time, number—are biological mutations fostered by evolution.[18] Dewey himself would apply physical theory unhesitatingly to the theory of inquiry if he saw a way.[19] Now there is really no inconsistency here. James and Dewey could view science as literally false on ontological points, but still they took it seriously as conceptual shorthand; and then they could reasonably ask, in the very terms of this conceptual shorthand, how men came to construct it. They could take a naturalistic, genetic epistemology as seriously as they took the rest of science.

Naturalism can show itself also in fallibilism. If with naturalism you forswear the ideal of a first philosophy, and if, in addition, you forswear analyticity, then fallibilism comes easily. For whatever reason, fallibilism was endemic among the pragmatists. Dewey, White tells us,[20] scotched the quest for certainty. But fallibilism in Peirce and James had a basis unrelated to naturalism. They believed in an element of absolute chance: that the future was uncertain in principle.

Peirce was decidedly naturalistic, however, in repudiating Cartesian doubt. We should recognize that we are born into a going conceptual scheme, he held; and we should work critically within it, doubting when conflicts arise.[21] Peirce scored a major point for naturalism, moreover, in envisioning a behavioristic semantics. Naturalism in psychology and semantics is behaviorism; and Peirce declared for such a semantics when he declared that beliefs consist in dispositions to action.

The doctrine has its attractions. If we were to ascribe beliefs in the light merely of declarations, we would have the question of veracity to reckon with. The behavioral approach by-passes that. Also it by-passes the problem of interpreting the believer's words, which he may mean differently from the way we would mean them. Moreover, if a behavioral theory accommodated beliefs generally, it would explain sentence meanings generally; for as I remarked earlier, the meaning of a sentence could be said to comprise the dispositions to action that would constitute belief in the truth of the sentence.

Any general theory of belief *or* of sentence meanings, along these lines, is of course moonshine—to borrow an epithet from James. Dispositions to behavior are of very limited service as criteria of belief. What behavior manifests my belief that Brutus killed Caesar? We must not include verbal behavior here, or the behavioral doctrine of belief loses its point.[22] Furthermore, even in cases where we can sensibly speak of taking some nonverbal action on the strength of a belief, there is generally no clear way to ascertain the belief from the action; for there will commonly be a complex of contributory beliefs, some supporting others. We can ascertain belief from action in primitive cases, where theory is at a minimum. Elsewhere, action evinces specific beliefs only when generously eked out with verbal testimony.

Evidently Peirce's behavioral account of belief is not one to rest with. There is no hope of carrying it out sentence by sentence. What is laudable about it is just its behaviorist spirit. Peirce made a general and explicit declaration for behaviorism, indeed, in the following terms: "We have no power of Introspection, but all knowledge of the internal world is derived by hypothetical reasoning from our knowledge of external facts."[23] This spirit reappears with new vigor in Mead's philosophy and psychology, and also in Dewey's semantics. Dewey long preceded Wittgenstein in insisting that there is no more to meaning than is to be found in the social use of linguistic forms.[24]

I could have listed behavioristic semantics as a sixth great step of post-Humean empiricism. I did not do so because I see it as integral to naturalism. Yet Comte, who preached naturalism, stopped short of behavioristic semantics. The credit must go to the pragmatists.

It is significant that Charles Morris, who was a disciple of the pragmatist Mead, chose the word 'pragmatics' for the behavioral end of the study of language. I am encouraged to think that behavioristic semantics is as distinctive a trait of pragmatism as any; and, indeed, Morris has asserted as much.[25] Certainly it is a trait that I applaud. It long since separated me from the logical positivists. But the term 'pragmatism' is of little service as an alternative name for this one trait.

The professing pragmatists do not relate significantly to what I took to be the five turning points in post-Humean empiricism. Tooke's shift from ideas to words, and Bentham's from words to sentences, were not detectable in Peirce's pragmatic maxim, but we found Peirce's further semantic discussions to be sentence-oriented in implicit ways. Peirce seemed at odds with Duhem's sytem-centered view, until we got to Peirce's theory of truth; but this we found unacceptable. Other pragmatists were sentence-oriented in an implicit way, but still at odds with the system-centered view, until we made hypothetico-deductive sense of Schiller's humanism. On the analytic-synthetic distinction, and on naturalism, the pragmatists blew hot and cold.

Thayer tried to formulate the distinctive tenets of pragmatism,[26] but the result was complex, and to make it come out right he had to pad his roster with some honorary pragmatists. In limiting my attention to the card-carriers, I have found little in the way of shared and distinctive tenets. The two best guesses seemed to be behavioristic semantics, which I so heartily approve, and the doctrine of man as truth-maker, which I share in large measure.

W. V. Quine

NOTES

1. Cf. C. K. Ogden, *Bentham's Theory of Fictions* (London: K. Paul, Trench, Trubner & Co., Ltd., 1932).
2. Whitehead and Russell, *Principia Mathematica*, 2nd edition (Cambridge: Cambridge University Press, 1925-27), Vol. 1, p. 24.
3. Charles Sanders Peirce, *Collected Papers* (Cambridge, Mass.: Harvard University Press, 1931-58), 5:402.
4. Ibid., 5:491.
5. Ibid., 5:412.
6. Ibid., 8:191.
7. This difficulty is noted by Israel Scheffler, *Four Pragmatists* (New York: Humanities Press, 1974), p. 81.
8. A. J. Ayer, *The Origins of Pragmatism* (San Francisco: Freeman, Cooper & Company, 1968), p. 27.
9. Peirce, *Collected Papers*, 6:480.
10. Ibid., 5:536.
11. William James, *Collected Essays and Reviews* (New York: Longmans, Green and Co., 1920), p. 412.
12. Charles Morris, *The Pragmatic Movement in American Philosophy* (New York: George Braziller, Inc., 1970), p. 61; Ralph Barton Perry, *The Thought and Character of William James* (Boston: Little Brown & Co., Inc., 1935), Vol. 2, p. 481.
13. F. C. S. Schiller, "William James and the Making of Pragmatism," *The Personalist*, 8(1927), pp. 81-93.
14. H. S. Thayer, *Meaning and Action: A Critical History of Pragmatism* (Indianapolis: The Bobbs-Merrill Co., 1968), pp. 286 ff.
15. Ernest Nagel, "Dewey's Theory of Natural Science, " in Sidney Hook, ed., *John Dewey: Philosopher of Science and Freedom* (New York: The Dial Press, 1950), p. 240.
16. *See* Morris, op. cit., pp. 72 ff.
17. Morton White, "Pragmatism and the Scope of Science," in Arthur Schlesinger, Jr., and Morton White, eds., *Paths of American Thought* (Boston: Houghton Mifflin Co., 1963), p. 201.
18. John Dewey, "The Development of American Pragmatism," *Studies in the History of Ideas* (New York: Columbia University Press, 1925), Vol. 2, pp. 370-71.
19. Felix Kaufmann, "John Dewey's Theory of Inquiry," in Hook, op. cit., p. 220.
20. Schlesinger and White, op. cit., p. 200.
21. Peirce, *Collected Papers*, 5:265.
22. Ibid., 5:416.
23. Ibid., 5:265.

24. John Dewey, *Experience and Nature* (Chicago: Open Court, 1925), p. 179.
25. Op. cit., p. 40.
26. Op. cit., p. 431.

PRAGMATISM
AND THE IMPORTANCE OF
BEING EARNEST

ERNEST GELLNER

THERE IS THE OFT QUOTED REMARK about the man who tried to be a philosopher, but cheerfulness kept breaking through.... What is less well known is the end of the story. He found a way out. He became a pragmatist. Thereafter, he was both a philosopher *and* cheerful.

A certain cheerfulness seems to be of the very essence of pragmatism, and is in effect one of its defining traits. Moreover, it seems to me a crucial error. It is not my wish to argue that a deep gloom is an absolute precondition of philosophic truth. Rather, a kind of pervasive *Angst* is a precondition of the correct formulation of the epistemic question. When it is absent, a missing of the point, a begging of the question, if not outright formal error, are the inescapable consequences.

As I hold this to be the central weakness of pragmatism, I am very pleased that Professor Quine's admirable paper itself highlights the trait, albeit in a deceptively *en passant* manner. Commenting on the difference between the views of the pragmatist F.C.S. Schiller and those of Sir Karl Popper, Quine suggests that Schiller's "doctrine of 'postulation,' which has us believing whatever we wish were true until it proves troublesome"[1] is very much the same as the hypothetico-deductive method commended and described by Popper, *"apart from an indefinable element of fun"*[2] (italics mine). Pragmatists are fun people, that much is clear.

Earlier in the same essay, this Joyful Science had already made its appearance, *nur mit ein bisschen anderen Worten*. Discussing the sources of pragmatist naturalism—which Quine rightly lists as one of its defining traits—he observes that "The other...source of naturalism is unregenerate realism, the robust state of mind of the natural scientist who has never felt any qualms beyond the negotiable uncertainties internal to science."[3]

It is this robust lack of any qualms such as would be discontinuous with the day-to-day ordinary working doubts inside science, which Quine commends, and considers both salutary and inherent in pragmatism. I entirely accept his diagnosis. This is indeed central to the position under discussion. We disagree only in its evaluation.

Now if we accept this self-characterization of pragmatism, and at the same time hold pragmatism to be in error, precisely in its addition to cheerfulness, does this mean that we hold gloom to be philosophically mandatory? Not exactly. Gloom may indeed be a decorous state of mind, and one befitting a man of sense, learning, and dignity. Nevertheless, it seems to me philosophically optional, and I for one should strongly oppose making it a necessary condition for senior appointments in philosophy.

Rather, the point is this: the relevant antithesis of cheerfulness is not gloom, but a sense of crisis. Crisis, in turn, must be distinguished from a problem. The distinction is: a problem is a difficulty which may well be serious and the solution of which may call for the utmost exertions, and which may be prolonged and arduous, but which, for all that, does not call for a reevaluation of the very criteria of what is to count as a solution, for any overall reassessment of all the criteria of solutions themselves. This difference has something in common with the distinction once upon a time propounded by the existentialist philosopher Gabriel Marcel between a problem and a mystery—where the latter is not simply a more difficult variant of the former, but qualitatively distinct because it involves the very relationship of the self to the object of inquiry. The failure to draw this distinction forcefully enough is also present in Popper's philosophy of science. Popper likes to insist that science consists of the solution of problems (and hence, incidentally, is continuous with evolutionary advances). The stress on solving problems is of course intended to bring out the contrast with the rival and rejected view of science as information-accumulation. But the notion of 'problem' faces two ways: it must be contrasted not merely with data-collection, but also with a crisis in which one no longer knows what is to count as problem and what is to count as a solution. For such situations, the twin injunctions—solve problems, criticize solutions—are no longer adequate. Talk of 'problems' prejudges too much, and does so on the optimistic, complacent side. Equally the difference has some affinity with the recently fashionable distinction between problems in normal science, on the one hand, and paradigm shifts, on the other. One's ultimate criteria of what is acceptable and what is problematic are intimately linked to one's very identity.

We can now also refine the concept of cheerfulness. Kant observed that love as a feeling cannot be commanded, and similarly, cheerfulness as a simple affect can hardly be prescribed. To do so would be both illiberal and pointless. If cheerfulness does indeed keep breaking through, why repress it? Why indeed. But it is not cheerfulness as a simple affect which concerns us. Rather it is cheerfulness as a strategy or style: that celebrated willingness to try and use any tool that is at hand, inspired by a confident expectation that though any one tool or effort may fail, by and large, one's kit contains adequate tools, that all in all our criteria are sound. It is this set of assumptions which really constitutes cheerfulness in the relevant cognitive sense. By contrast, it is their suspension which constitutes a crisis.

Thus pragmatism stands for cheerfulness, as defined, in opposition to a sense of crisis. But it also generally stands for a resolutely third-person idiom, as opposed to the first-person style characteristic of classical epistemology and of radical empiricism. In fact, it is arguable that what distinguishes pragmatism from radical empiricism is precisely this trait: that it is a kind of externalization, objectification of empiricism or sensationalism. Such externalization certainly is commended to Professor Quine, as he makes plain in a number of contexts. The transition from talking about *ideas* to talking about *words*, which he commends in the present essay, is of course one version of it. A very great deal hinges, of course, on whether one uses a third- or a first-person idiom. Each of these idioms sums up, embodies, an entire philosophic program and attitude.

Radical empiricism in effect asserts that all true statements about the world are ultimately statable in the first person. *Esse est percipi*. To be is to be perceived: to be perceived is to be perceived by *someone*. A fact is an account of someone's perception. Someone has to be able to say, with truth, "I perceive...." Even if other forms of speech occur and omit this locution, it is always tacitly present if the assertion is true and warranted. This makes the perceiving subject ultimate and distinctive. It is he who examines the data and constructs the world, a world, out of them. In skeptical mood, he may wonder whether the data really and truly add up to a usable world. But the ego comes first, and the world is constructed from the data it has received.

A totally different vision is implied in the use of the third person as fundamental. *I* can stand outside the world; *he* cannot. There are certain irregular expressions. ("I am Oxford; you are Cambridge; he is London School of Economics.") These also occur in philosophy. "I construct the world, him included," is acceptable. "He constructs the world, me included," is not. The use of *he* firmly places the cognizing person or organism in the context of other things and other centers of consciousness, and deprives him and his cognitive enterprise of any privileged, external, extraterritorial status. The third person is Copernican. If we insist on doing epistemology in the third person, as Quine does, we thereby firmly presuppose a public world within which both the process of cognition and the organism benefiting from it stand alongside other things and other processes, not radically distinct from them, and unable to claim any special status.

The question now arises—which of these two idioms is really fundamental, ultimate, justified?

It would seem that we are in the presence of a stalemate, insofar as each of them appears to possess knock-down arguments for the elimination of its rival.

The argument for the exclusion of the third-person viewpoint or terminology is above all an entirely cogent appeal against *begging of the question*. It runs as follows: if the theory of knowledge is to be discussed at all, its conclusion must not be prejudged, as indeed is mandatory for any other genuine inquiry. If you ask a question at all, if you hold it worth asking, then it must be decided in the light of the evidence adduced, rather than prejudged. It is no use having a debate like the one between the medieval king and the Jew about the merits of their respective religions, which had to be carried on on the assumption of the validity of the king's faith. The issue in epistemology is what and *whether* we know; and one possible answer must be that we do *not*. But the whole use of the third-person idiom is simply a camouflaged—and not even very cunningly camouflaged—assumption that we *do* know the world which we think we know, that it is roughly as we always supposed, and that *within* it, we can find out just how we came to know what we do know anyway.... This is childishly circular reasoning. Quine endorses it, knowingly and with defiance, and he resolutely spurns the use of camouflage.

There is no shadow of doubt in my mind that the charge of childish circularity of reasoning is established up to the hilt. It is, of course, possible to call it 'robust' or 'fun'—and, no doubt, it qualifies under either heading. But can you really establish a philosophy by stressing that it is held by robust healthy people, when that very philosophy is also allowed to decide what is healthy?

Unfortunately, the rival position is just as vulnerable. The attack against it can be formulated as follows: the first person philosophy assumes a self-prior-to-the-world, which chooses whether or not graciously to allow itself to be persuaded of the reality of the world. But every tool—sensory, conceptual, linguistic, physiological—which it employs in its deliberations is part and parcel of that very world which it would judge and 'suspend'! Alternatively, even if this philosophy does not literally believe in a prior-self, it supposes at least that the skeptical cognitive Hamlet can propel himself into a kind of cosmic exile...but is this not absurd?

There are various ways of demonstrating the hubris, the absurdity of such a pretension. The way evidently much favored by Quine, and many others, is from the failure to find a way of characterizing 'pure data,' which would furnish our Hamlet's mind in his extraterrestrial exile, and which would avoid being saturated by theories drawn from *within* that world which had supposedly been 'suspended'.

There are other ways of attaining the desired conclusion. A recently fashionable one is to insist that any identification or sense of that very 'self' which is to observe its own 'data' is contingent on the practical activity by that self in the world, and thus that world is surreptitiously presupposed as soon as we speak of the self at all. I think—therefore *the world* is. Or again, the linguistic philosophers did it through their putative proof that there could be no private language. If so, all languages are necessarily public. Hence, the very speech in which you query the reality of the public world, already presupposes it! We speak, hence the world is. I well remember one such thinker, arguing that solipsism was possible for animals, but not for language-endowed men. Speech guaranteed the world.... How simple. Or again, the very act of thought presupposes a conceptual and linguistic system of great complexity—whose rules are not even known to the individual operating it, let alone chosen or made by him. These systems can only exist in the world and are sustained by it. They cannot pretend to exist independently, nor can that thought which is only articulated through them.

So be it. I for one do not wish to dispute the conclusive force of these arguments, which I have somewhat informally sketched out. But if the conclusive force of destructive arguments on each side is conceded, where does this leave us?

The situation is indeed a stalemate. I do not believe that it has any resolution, if we consider the third-/first-person issue in isolation. But each side of this opposition is intimately and inescapably linked to our initial contrast between cheerfulness and sense of crisis. The third-person view is linked to cheerfulness: if the world and its general outlines, and the outlines of what counts as the solution of problems, are all given, then indeed we are only faced with specific problems rather than with an overall crisis. Conversely, a sense of pervasive crisis calls for a radical and *general* reassessment, and this generality can only be genuine if attained without question-begging, and if it proceeds from some independent, external stance.

In other words, the two visions are tied to two alternative possible situations; and hence, by considering our situation within the world (as indeed the third-person theorists would have us do anyway), we may, in a way, decide, not so much which of the two visions is correct, but which is mandatory. Thus, in a sense, we are, at least experimentally, playing by third-person rules.

We must now look within that given world to see what our situation is really like. Note that, though in one way we are playing the game by third-person rules, in another sense the cards are also somewhat stacked against that position. To achieve victory, the first-person position does not need to establish that the human situation is permanently and everywhere in a state of crisis. Such a claim would in any case be absurd, and were it true, our position would presumably be beyond either help or solution. All the first-person theorist in fact requires is that *sometimes,* at crucial times, conditions resemble that which we have defined as crisis.

This brings us to the next polarity, which separates pragmatists and their opponents, and which concerns the area from which evidence, and above all the basic image, is drawn. Pragmatism is inspired by two areas: biology (Darwinism, evolutionism), and by nineteenth-century socioeconomic and intellectual history. These two in many ways incomparable and disparate regions nevertheless have some crucial traits in common. Each of them seems at least to have been a success story. In each case, the success seems to have been unplanned, and attained by uncoordinated or even in the main unconscious individual effort, by repeated trial-and-error, by endeavor which does not spurn the successive utilization of quite diverse methods or paths, and which receives both its impetus and its checks in the hurly-burly of concrete struggle. Marx planned to dedicate one of his works to Darwin, in ironical spirit as S. Avineri has pointed out, as a comment on the manner in which nineteenth-century laissez-faire capitalism delighted to find a parable or confirmation in Darwinian nature.

The pragmatists were not necessarily or all of them social Darwinists:

...not all Americans who admired evolutionary thought derived from it...laissez–faire conclusions....many American thinkers dissented from the social doctrines of Sumner and Herbert Spencer, for example...John Dewey. ...Dewey's variety of pragmatism was probably more distinguished and more lasting in its influence than any of the other American movements affected by evolutionary doctrine....[4]

Some of them were, of course: the analogy between the alleged improvement of biological species and the improvement of the human stock of ideas, institutions, and indeed of the human stock itself, is too tempting, whether or not it is really defensible. But whether or not progress hinges on *competition,* there are also other links between the two visions. There are many witnesses: "...William James, occasionally spoke of his theory of mind as a corollary of Darwinian biology...."[5]

Pragmatism emphasized not the brute hardness of things transparently evident to consciousness, but rather the control of an organism's conceptions by its actions and their connected consequence in experience. It demanded that speculative abstractions be rejected as meaningless unless they could be reconstructed as predicting differential sensible outcomes of specified operations. It insisted, further, that truths acquired their warrant through publicly verifiable anticipation of the course of experience, contingent upon human transformation of the environment.[6]

In his psychological writings, James consistently presents the facts of mental life...always in the most intimate relations to men's biological needs and functions, and the constant task of adaptation with which every organism is faced. When he turned from psychology to philosophy...he passed to the more exciting...thesis that the sole function of thought is to satisfy certain interests of the organism, and that truth consists in such thinking as satisfies these interests.[7]

Various facets of the pragmatic response....A dominant theme is the *rejection of Cartesian thought*....Flowing from this rejection are several pragmatic emphases...: the *functional view of thought*, relating cognition to the biological, social, and purposive life of the organism; the *fallibilistic view of knowledge*...; the *social and experimental conception of science*...; and the *representative character of thinking*....

The interpretation of *thought as intimately interwoven with action* in a purposive context is stressed by pragmatism as indicating the *continuity of mind and nature*: the mind acquires knowledge through physical interactions with its environment....[8]

Pragmatism [is]: A theory of knowledge, experience and reality maintaining...that thought and knowledge are biologically and socially evolved modes of adaptation to and control over experience and reality.... The ways in which experience is apprehended, systematized, and anticipated may be many. Here pragmatism counsels tolerance and pluralism. But...all theorizing is subject to the critical objective of maximum usefulness in serving our needs....[9]

The biological vision reinforced the third-person view: the biological vision could not even be articulated unless we were first granted an external world as its arena. And there are other connections: the optimistic expectation of long-term improvement, the stress on ordeal by practice rather than by confrontation with some abstract ideal, the expectation and high valuation of concrete diversity, and so forth.

It is of course possible to attack this Continuity Thesis, so to speak, between biological and human history; and moreover, it is possible to attack it from two quite different sides, each of which is highly relevant, though in different ways.

One argument starts from the fact that both biological evolution and industrial-economic history of the nineteenth century (allowing for a moment that the analogy between the two of them is valid) are most untypical of the rest of human history proper. Each of them exhibits both instability and growth, albeit in one case this can only be detected at the scale of millions of years, whilst in the other it can be discerned by the participants and so to speak with the naked eye. But in fact the characteristic condition of a very great deal of human history is either stalemate-equilibrium or acute crisis. Sustained growth is, alas, untypical. Many social forms, notably oriental civilizations, have persisted over many centuries and appear to possess mechanisms for avoiding radical change; elsewhere, violent crises have totally shaken social systems in such a way that the criteria of survival themselves have undergone radical transformation within them.

The examples of cognitive growth favored by a pragmatist such as Quine seem to be drawn precisely from these two areas—from biological, organic adaptation, or on the other hand, from within a scientific discipline within which overall criteria are reasonably clear, consensual, and established. We have already stressed the pragmatist failure to consider crisis and radical discontinuity, and this is indeed the crucial and *decisive* weakness of pragmatism. But in a different way, the blindness to (from our viewpoint) excessive stability, to the self-maintaining rigor mortis of so many social and intellectual systems, is also a very grave weakness, and the complement of the other one. These two blindnesses or insensitivities are correlative. Fundamental crisis characteristically occurs when one of these self-maintaining systems collapses, whether through internal stress or external impact, and then becomes incapable of coping at all.

There is, of course, something paradoxical in speaking of biological history and its pattern as 'untypical': within its own terms and area, it must, of course, be the very norm of typicality. For a variety of reasons, it just happens to be a bad analogy or parable for human history. But the other region in time and space which specially inspired the pragmatists—the economic history of nineteenth-century America, plus those other countries that passably resemble it—is, of course, highly untypical of human history, and to try and extract a universal philosophy from its underlying spirit is somewhat absurd. At some levels, thinkers like William James must have been aware of this, precisely insofar as they thought they were formulating a distinctively American philosophy, and one based on the American experience. At the same time, he was clearly willing to see it used for export. Presumably he believed that though all men are human, Americans are more so, that the American experience is more paradigmatically human.[10]

But it is not the special temporal narrowness of the evidence alone that counts against it. One may also question whether the material has been correctly interpreted. A naive adherent of laissez-faire, contemplating late nineteenth-century America, might well conclude that economic competition is, on its own, the secret of economic growth at any time and in any place. Similarly, an epistemologist might in analogous circumstances conclude that intellectual competition and pragmatic trial-and-error will automatically lead to cognitive growth. In fact, in either case, the miracle only works in the right climate—whether political or intellectual.

It is precisely the once-and-for-all establishment of this climate, after some stagnant stalemate or general crisis, which is the *real* secret; but individuals or societies happily born long after the firm and confident establishment of such a climate, may simply take it for granted, and be ever inclined to think of it, not as *one* social climate amongst others, but as the natural and well-nigh inevitable condition of mankind. (Such a mentality underlies pragmatism.) A society like that simply does not remember any *ancien régime*. Even if they know intellectually that things had once been very different, they may have some difficulty in really feeling it. Traits which elsewhere are antitraditional, "radical," are part and parcel of American tradition itself. As Bernard Crick puts it,

> American politics...are almost inescapably 'Lockean.' They exhibit...a purely utilitarian and contractual view of government....But all this, while

making Lockean whiggery still the clearest political sociology of American life, is still a Lockeanism that never had to struggle against an *ancien régime*. For the 'American Revolution' was never a revolution at all in the meaning of that term that has dominated European politics since 1789. "The great advantage of the American," Hartz quotes De Tocqueville, "is that he has arrived at a state of democracy without having to endure a democratic revolution: and that he is born equal without having to become so."[11]

The mistaken supposition that a given environment, in fact historically most specific, is inherent in the very nature of things, *did* receive much encouragement from a questionable reading of biological history. In brief, the mind of a pragmatist turns easily to Atlantic economic history of the nineteenth century, or the history of science *after* the seventeenth century, or to the evolution of the whole species; but one does not often see it lingering on the ancient Near East, on the Middle Ages, or on Chinese, Hindu, or Muslim civilization.[12]

But—to reach the next point—is there in fact any continuity between biological evolution and cognitive growth? Let us leave aside the well-known and oft-noted differences between genetic and social transmission of information, with all that this implies. There is another highly significant difference. Natural selection selects through survival by a *multiplicity* of diverse criteria, and at the same time each of these criteria only operates concretely, in a definite and well-defined context. They do not, so to speak, extrapolate to hypothetical contexts. Candidates are eliminated only by real, not by hypothetical ordeals. The animal must be brave enough to repel attackers who can be repelled, yet sufficiently fleet of foot to flee from strong ones, and clever enough to distinguish the two, etc., etc. At the same time, the specific nature of these ordeals ensures that natural selection only molds the species for the context in which it actually finds itself; it does not and cannot, as it were, train it for environments which it has not yet encountered. It cannot, as it were, act at a distance or in anticipation. An ordeal will eliminate those who fail that particular ordeal and that particular ordeal only; it will not prepare an organism for future and different ordeals.

There is an enormous difference between an organ or an organism and a proposition or theory. An organ can in a sense be said to embody an anticipation: the giraffe's neck embodies the assumption of the availability of nourishment some distance above ground and out of the reach of ordinary necks. The consequent survival of animals endowed with long necks constitutes a kind of confirmation of that unspoken anticipation, whilst their elimination might be its falsification—but only with tremendous qualifications. The world is full of creatures with dismally short necks, or even no necks to speak of. More important, animals with unduly long necks might be eliminated not because the tacit anticipation of food-at-height is false, but because the anatomical consequences of excessive neck lengths are unfavorable. Organs survive not merely because of the truth or falsity of the anticipations which can be said to be tacitly contained in them, but because of their effects on the whole assembly of organs, on the organism.

By contrast (and *pace* Quine), propositions possess relatively definite and circumscribed meanings or 'anticipations.' They stand or fall by what they *say* rather than by their side-effects. Quine, of course, likes to insist on their esprit de corps, on how they stand and fall as corporate units, how failure in one place can lead to adjustments elsewhere in the system and so forth. But this diffuseness of meaning is a matter of degree. The very fact that we can often identify the one place in which failure occurred, the fact that we can translate from language to language (though, of course, this very consideration leads Quine to be skeptical of translations), shows that propositions have become individualistic to a most remarkable degree. (Not completely, of course.) And I believe that it is this very fact of relatively isolable meaning, of *not* facing reality as a corporate body, which is precisely what is responsible in large measure for the amazing cognitive growth of modern times. There is, of course, in human societies something analogous to the way in which organs stand and fall together, in clusters, and not by the merit of the 'anticipations' seen in isolation: it is found in traditional societies, which have belief systems so intertwined with the status and authority structures of their culture that nothing important can change without imperiling the rest, and hence most parts are systematically protected. The liberation of propositions from this collective responsibility—a liberation which I admit is not total—is, I suspect, one of the distinctive features of the scientific spirit, which helps to account for its success, and which, at the same time, precludes the application of the same principle to biological adaptation and to scientific growth.

Quine's celebrated holism is moreover in implicit conflict with his evolutionism. Natural selection can only operate on reasonably large species, subjected to a fairly steady environment for some goodly length of time. Human history fulfills none of these conditions: a relatively small number of cultures, so small at the later stages that luck must play a big part in deciding who wins and survives, have competed over a fairly short period of time, in a social environment so unstable in the later period that all conclusions are perilous. (Are the institutions chosen by natural selection in the nineteenth century the ones most fit to serve in the twentieth?) By insisting on holism, on the mutual confrontation of enormous intellectual systems, rather than of isolated statements, Quine in effect makes sure that the number of competing entrants in this selective game is so small that victory ceases to be statistically significant. The collectivism, the sharing of responsibility, would lead to the swamping of any advantageous innovations and to the protection of cognitive lame ducks. The collectives, on the other hand, are so small in number that their "selection" by history must be strongly affected by accident rather than by fitness, whatever fitness may be.

Now consider that mysterious entity we call truth, or whatever it is which so very visibly augments during periods of marked cognitive growth, i.e., in the course of the history of modern science. It does *not* satisfy a wide multiplicity of criteria but, on the contrary, a rather narrow range of them, or perhaps even just a single criterion; and it is also conspicuously extrapolative. To put it in more concrete terms: what distinguishes the scientific thought style from pre-scientific ones is notably the fact that instead of satisfying *many* criteria—including social cohesion, authority-maintenance, morale, etc.—it sheds all but one aim, i.e., explanatory power and congruence with facts.[13] Moreover, far from adapting to one specific environment—which is the only aim that natural selection can serve—it endeavors to cover as wide a range of environments, of situations, as possible, and so to speak to seek them out actively in the process of testing, rather than waiting till *they* test *it*.

In somewhat different words, this point has often been raised against pragmatism. Pragmatism assimilates truth to that which is useful. Thereby, in effect, it conflates that which is useful because it is true (it is useful to know that there is a precipice ahead, because there is indeed a precipice there) and that which is useful *for other reasons*, independent of or even opposed to truth. It may be useful not to be apprehensive about precipices, because it sustains one's endeavors, for instance.

Pragmatism was encouraged in this conflation by various considerations, including the notorious difficulty of defining truth in a noncircular or non-nebulous manner. Usefulness appeared a way out of this difficulty, and one which moreover avoided any need to step outside experience. The conflation has numerous and, I suspect, insuperable difficulties of its own, such as that of defining the range, i.e., the time-span and the number of individuals who are to be taken into consideration when 'usefulness' is assessed. But these problems are well known and there is no need to dwell on them once again. What is important here is to stress the pragmatist failure to appreciate the real significance of the contrast between serving *many* ends and serving *one* restricted and clearly specified end.

Old pragmatism was blinded by its conflict with Hegelianism and the Hegelian pursuit of the One, of the great unity (whether in things or in selecting aims), and consequently it simply loved to dwell on the tangled multiplicity of ends in real life. This is indeed so—life is complex—and pragmatists were perhaps closer to 'real life' than Hegelians. But this is *not* the way in which the one-many opposition hits the problem of knowledge.

Knowledge, even more than other forms of production perhaps, hinges on the division of labor and the separation of functions. Scientific thought is distinct from prescientific forms of adaptation by being subjected to *one* and not to multiple criteria, or at least to a highly delimited set of criteria (compatibility with what is established, elegance and simplicity, extension to new areas). Moreover it contains an in-built tendency to extrapolate its findings to areas in which 'the environment' is as yet making no impact on the organism or community in question—whereas of course blind, unconscious natural selection can only respond to an environment that is actually making an impact. Science is, so to speak, gratuitously provocative. The nearest thing which may modify this picture is that evolution sometimes also selects for an unspecified general adaptability, as opposed to specific adaptation—in other words for intelligence.

But, insofar as this free-ranging adaptability serves the multiple ends of adaptation, it will still be quite distinct from the relatively single-purpose pursuit of truth. Concretely, the fruits of prescientific human intelligence may often have been much richer than those of the relatively austere scientific spirit: the art and culture of some prescientific civilizations may well be more exciting than the art and culture of scientific ones. "What James looked for, and indeed found partial proof of... was support for his own native conviction that the universe is an infinitely richer, warmer, more varied and indeed more 'jumpy' place than nineteenth-century materialist doctrines would have us believe...."[14] It is also probably true that such a free-ranging adaptability, which may correspond fairly closely to what is normally termed intelligence, must have been a precondition to the scientific spirit, and also that it may itself have been produced simply by the play of natural selection. But this does not make natural selection and the scientific spirit identical. The turn it has taken when it became science is neither itself dictated by natural selection—how much for humanity's chances of survival now?—nor does it, in the new austere blinkered restriction of its aims, simply exemplify adaptability as such. It is quite distinct.

So pragmatism has indeed stumbled on an important binary opposition in its interest in the contrast between pluralism and monism of aims, but its tie-up of truth—at any rate of scientific truth—with pluralism is a veritable inversion of the real state of affairs. Natural selection operates by bombarding its candidates from a wide variety of angles and subjecting them to a great variety of tests. It thus selects for a great multiplicity of 'virtues.' Modern cognitive growth, on the other hand, selects only for a very restricted range of qualities. The idea that these qualities make for survival is highly questionable and certainly unproven.

The pluralism that pragmatism values is intimately connected with another important trait, namely its rejection of discontinuities. Its opponents like to insist on some pretty fundamental, radical ditches in reality: pragmatists, on the other hand, are skeptical of such dualisms. We have seen that they characteristically insist on what may be called the Continuity Thesis concerning biological evolution and the growth of human knowledge; but they are just as keen in the continuity between commonsensical knowledge and scientific knowledge, between science and philosophy, between cognition and evaluation, between truths of reason and matters of fact, between formal and substantive knowledge. The denial of dichotomies seems to be distinctly habit-forming:

> John Dewey has spent a good part of his life hunting and shooting at dualisms: body-mind, theory-practice, percept-concept, value-science, learning-doing, sensation-thought, external-internal. They are always fair game and Dewey's prose rattles with fire whenever they come into view. At times the philosophical forest seems more like a gambler at a penny arcade, and the dualist dragons move along obligingly and monotonously while Dewey picks them off with deadly accuracy.[15]

There is indeed a kind of affinity, at the very least, between this trait and the pragmatist's other choices in the various binary alternatives we have drawn. For one thing, there is a connection between the pluralism, the insistence on so many diverse ploys and aims, and this feature: many small distinctions as it were drown the big ones which thus disappear. All the small distinctions count, but they do not allow a few of their own number to dominate.

There are also other connections. The Big Divides were characteristically used as the principal means of articulating the Cosmic Exile, of attaining the external, extraterritorial stance from which cognition was to be validated, and in terms of which its Fundamental Constitutional Law of Knowledge was to be drawn up. Pragmatism denies either the need or the feasibility of such a Prior Philosophy, and is naturally suspicious of the conceptual devices which seem to make it possible. If Big Divides help to formulate a Prior Philosophy, that only reinforces the suspicion in which they are held. William James, in *Pragmatism,* spoke critically of idealist philosophy as a kind of Shining Temple on a Hill, the simple classical lines of which bore little resemblance to the tangled complexity of real life. In Quine's hands, and perhaps before, pragmatism itself acquires this quality. The sense of continuity, the eager erosion of those 'dualisms' and radical discontinuities with which other philosophers operated, results in a curious standardization of everything, a new dusk in which all cows are the same shade of grey, in which all cognitive advances partake in the same status of corrigible adjustments in some big cognitive corporation. Small differences are not denied, of course, but being so small and numerous, like the petty shareholders in property-owning democracy, they cannot really defy the great organizations, those great 'corporate bodies,' that only face experience collectively.

I have now attempted both a characterization and a criticism of pragmatism, and the criticism, of course, hinges on the characterization. The characterization is expressed in terms of a whole series of linked binary oppositions, such that the pragmatist is he who thinks in terms of these oppositions, and makes his choices wholly or predominantly from one side of the barrier (See page 60.) The manner of setting out the situation, in fact, owes more to William James himself than to the recent *structuraliste* penchant for binary oppositions. But unlike James's list of tender-minded and tough-minded traits, which of course inspires my approach, this is not meant to be an overall typology of human beings or of styles of thought. On the contrary, I hold this particular series of contrasts, and many of the links between them, to be historically most specific, to arise in a particular social and intellectual situation—but it is precisely in that situation that pragmatism is born, and pragmatism is basically a name for that cluster of choices in that series of alternatives.

So much for a characterization, which of course was meant to be as fair and unprejudiced as I could make it, and to bring out the underlying feel and force of both positions. There is an interesting

Ernest Gellner

Pragmatist	Anti-Pragmatist
Cheerful, in the sense of willing to proceed in a happy-go-lucky spirit, using any tool at hand, trusting own powers	Anxiety-imbued sense of crisis, which insists on circumspect and above all methodical inspection of any tools, lest they be contaminated
Hence pluralistic in aims and methods	Hence monistic or near-monistic
Hence inclined to seek continuities between biological and social history, philosophy and science, formal and substantive knowledge, etc.	Operates in terms of radical dichotomies
Critical of feasibility or need for 'cosmic exile,' 'prior philosophy'	Suspicious of current trends, hankers after external, independent validation
In this sense 'naturalistic'	Extra-natural vantage point sought
Favors third-person idiom	Drawn to ego—redoubt
Finds evidence of illustration in successful (or seemingly so) developments—biological evolution, history of science since seventeenth century, modern economic history	Sensitive to both the stagnant and cataclysmic periods of human history
Favors laissez-faire in intellectual sphere	Favors at least occasional intervention in name of fundamental principle, when threatened by chaos or stalemate

Importance of Being Earnest

difference between older pragmatism and Quine's, hinging on the fact that the earlier version was reacting primarily to the idealists, whereas the modern form is engaged in a debate with other empiricists. The current situation is enshrined in the very form of Quine's present essay, which asks, in effect—*within* our wider and shared empiricist faith—is pragmatism going the right way, or is it heretical?

Now the old idealists were themselves opposed to dualisms, notably of the Kantian kind. Hence, when they were inebriated by the Great Continuities, more sober men such as the pragmatists would be tempted to stress the idea of sensory evidence against them; hence that occasional inclination to first-person sensory language, rather than behaviorist talk, which Quine considers regretably regressive.

Neopositivism, on the other hand, used "sense data language" or equivalents as a tacitly extramundane stance from which to establish their position and damn others. Quine is concerned with this internal dispute between brother-empiricists rather than with the earlier one, which helps to explain distinctive traits of his particular version of the pragmatist syndrome. But now for the evaluation.

It seems to me that pragmatism is indefensible, because radical cataclysms do occur. When they do, cheerfulness, in the sense defined—a happy reliance on the existing stock of tools and ideas, without any effort at a prior philosophy—simply is not a workable strategy. The pragmatist illusion that it *is* viable springs from an unacknowledged—and indeed unconscious—reliance on previous and successful efforts by 'prior philosophers' to clear the ground in such crises, and it is unwittingly parasitic on them. Pragmatism is distinctively American—not, as is sometimes wrongly suggested, in that it seems to ratify some specific form of economic organization or ethos, but in that it emerged within a society which takes cognitive growth altogether for granted; and it does this because it only came into being at a time when such growth had indeed become the norm. As Quine himself has it, "The naturalistic philosopher begins his reasoning with the inherited world theory *as a going concern*"[16] [italics mine]. But the inherited human world is generally nothing of the kind. When it *is* a going and growing concern, that is a highly idiosyncratic, miraculous and most fortunate condition. It needs to be understood and explained, rather than invoked as a reason for why no explanation is required at all. But that is what the denial of the need for a 'prior philosophy' really amounts to. A 'prior philosophy' specifies and justifies the general traits or preconditions of cognitive growth *without* invoking an allegedly general, pervasive, natural process as the main explanation. The denial of a 'prior philosophy' hinges on a background theory (which in Quine's case, most laudably, is not tacit but is often avowed) about the overall natural process; and this background theory is false. By contrast, a 'prior philosophy,' rightly treating cognitive health as exceptional, must endeavor to stand outside nature in order to identify and to justify the healthy state. Cheerfulness—the reliance on a happy condition in which, all in all, the tools that are at hand can be trusted—is *no* substitute at all. It is incapable of identifying and selecting: it loves the lot, or at any rate, much too much of it.[17]

One might sum up all this by saying that it is a refutation of pragmatism by an argument from Max Weber. What really distinguishes Weber from nineteenth-century evolutionisms, of which pragmatism is a surviving example, is a strong sense of the *dis*continuity between the modern outlook and the past: a recognition that, contrary to the feelings of Hegelians, Marxists, Darwinists, and others, our outlook is not simply a refinement or perpetuation of what had been going on for a long, long time. On the contrary, it was, to speak in these terms, a remarkable mutation which need not really have happened at all and indeed could not have been expected to happen. It needs to be understood not by invoking the same principles as explain everything else, by saying this is just more of the same, but rather by isolating the specific causes, and traits, of something which historically is so *very* idiosyncratic.

Weber was not specially concerned with the history of epistemology, but it is a field in which his ideas have considerable application. The modern growth of knowledge is as dramatic, unique, and discontinuous with the past as is the modern productive style and economic organization. There are many obvious parallels between them. Modern post-Cartesian philosophy is, even or especially when it thinks it is dealing with knowledge in general and at all times, an attempt to understand, delimit and justify this unique cognitive development. Pragmatism is in error precisely because it does not consider it to be unique and consequently tries to explain it by invoking factors relevant at *all* times. This illusion springs from the fact that pragmatism was born so very much *within* this unique phenomenon that it takes it for granted, believes it to be universal, and really cannot conceive that things could be very different. The protestant work ethic, which appears in Quine as "scientific method," is taken as self-evident.

The idea that the world is so constructed that this ethic is also, by and large, rewarded, is likewise taken for granted. Quine is painfully caught between his naturalism (which is a kind of protestant egalitarianism—no one is allowed to give himself airs of standing outside nature) and his view of knowledge as man-made. The former leads to a certain realism, the latter to a subjectivism or idealism. I frankly do not understand how he thinks he can square these viewpoints, and the passages in which he claims to do so, such as a remarkable one in his present essay, seem to me brilliant displays of literary sleight-of-hand. At times, he also falls back on a coy and playful objectivism-through-ultra-subjectivism—*my* viewpoint is objective for me because obviously *I* cannot have anything else, so there. "We cannot talk otherwise." But just as characteristically, and more fundamentally, he falls back on this optimistic evolutionist background theory—the Holy Spirit under the name of Scientific Method is guiding us along the right path, so all's well, and no constitutional law is required for the Republic of learning—and this background theory is mistaken.

NOTES

1. W.V. Quine, "The Pragmatists' Place in Empiricism," this volume, p. 33.
2. Ibid.
3. Ibid., p. 28.
4. Cf. Morton White, *Pragmatism and the American Mind* (New York: Oxford University Press, 1973), pp. 194-95.

5. Morton White, op. cit., p. 96.
6. Israel Scheffler, *Science and Subjectivity* (Indianapolis: The Bobbs-Merrill Co., 1967), p. 4.
7. W. B. Gallie, *Peirce and Pragmatism* (Harmondsworth: Penguin Books, 1952), p. 25.
8. Israel Scheffler, *Four Pragmatists* (London: Routledge & Kegan Paul, Ltd., 1974), p. 8.
9. H.S. Thayer, *Meaning and Action. A Critical History of Pragmatism* (Indianapolis: The Bobbs-Merrill Co., 1968), p. 431.
10. Cf. W. James, *Pragmatism*, ch. 1.
11. "Liberalism Transplanted" in *The Twentieth Century*, June 1957, p. 529.
12. In explaining the strong reliance of pragmatism on the continuity thesis, I invoke the fact that American culture contains no folk memory of any *ancien régime*. (The American Revolution was a defense of the decencies which the continuity thesis underwrites, and not a defiant act of Reason against Tradition.) This is indeed so. At the same time it must be admitted that the continuity thesis is sometimes upheld by thinkers springing from cultures in which the *ancien régime* is vividly remembered—such as Sir Karl Popper with his doctrine that the amoeba was a good Popperite. Optimistic continuity theses, such as are found in Quine or in the later Popper, must of course be carefully distinguished from *static* optimistic background theories, which evoked, precisely, an idealized *ancien régime* as the guarantor of our cognitive endeavor, with some slogan such as that every form of life is valid, by its own lights, and that there can be no other.
13. Cf. Robin Horton, "African Traditional Thought and Western Science," *Africa*, Vol. XXXVII, April 1967, pp. 155-87.
14. W. B. Gallie, op. cit., p. 24.
15. Morton White, op. cit., pp. 121-22.
16. Quine, op. cit., p. 28.
17. Quine is, of course, a somewhat idiosyncratic pragmatist. His chief idiosyncratic trait arises from the fact that his vision is produced, so to speak, by the intersection of two distinct and mutually incommensurate reductionist programs—the naturalist (third-person) one and nominalism. It is this which gives that vision its singular quality, its so-to-speak Dali-esque flavor, or the sense of a montage resulting from the completion of two pictures in different dimensions, as it were. But his attitude to these two programs and hence their implementation are also quite different and unsymmetrical, and this adds to the sense of oddity. His implementation of naturalism is enthusiastic and less than fastidious—the transition from promise to execution is facile and none too scrupulous. The hope is easily mistaken for fulfillment, and if admissions are wrung from him about the failure to implement (for instance by Chomsky's points about the innate elements in language learning), one does not feel that

Importance of Being Earnest

the concessions are taken too seriously, or their implications fully appreciated. There seems to be a cheerful confidence that it will be all right on the night, that the programs must be sound, and never mind a few difficulties. By contrast, he is utterly sensitive and severely fastidious with respect to the execution of nominalism, and in fact his standards in this matter are unusually, perhaps uniquely, high. Moreover, his love of mathematics—and hence of the abstract entities which, according to him, it requires—makes him less than displeased if the nominalist program fails, as on his view it does. His logical fastidiousness and his ontological preference seem to converge at this point. All the same, one never knows which of the two programs is put into operation where, or why, or just how far it will be carried out. This gives Quine's world both its unpredictable and its odd character.

FROM CYNICISM TO AMELIORATION: STRATEGIES FOR A CULTURAL PEDAGOGY

JOHN J. McDERMOTT

INTRODUCTION

THE TERM AMERICAN PRAGMATISM cloaks a number of options when given as the title of a conference. One could approach it archivally and discuss the genesis of 'pragmatism' in the writings of Chauncey Wright, C. S. Peirce, William James, and John Dewey. Again the approach could involve an analysis of the epistemological claims consonant with pragmatism and perhaps an attempt to put them over against more contemporary positions. There is, however, still a third option available. Although I accept James's stricture that pragmatism is not so much a philosophy as a method, it is nonetheless true that the appellation 'American pragmatism' most often stands for American philosophy of the classical period, from 1870 to 1920. In this last sense, pragmatism becomes nothing less than a name for a distinct philosophical approach to a wide range of problems. William James says as much, when he writes:

There can *be* no difference anywhere that doesn't *make* a difference elsewhere—no difference in abstract truth that doesn't express itself in a difference in concrete fact and in conduct consequent upon that fact, imposed on somebody, somehow, somewhere and somewhen. The whole function of philosophy ought to be to find out what definite difference it will make to you and me, at definite instants of our life, if this world-formula or that world-formula be the true one.[1]

Now James, of course, has no "world-formula" and, indeed, only a page later, rails against "the pretence of finality in truth." What he is warning us against is that naivete, which assumes that our ideas and theories do not engender concrete differences in the actualities of our private lives. Taking this warning as indicative of the pragmatic temper, I have chosen to discuss and evaluate some of the regnant social theories of our time and then place against them the thought of John Dewey. I am not attempting simply to resuscitate the language and ideas of a previous generation, in order to provide a panacea. Rather, I believe that Dewey and the philosophical tradition he represents still has considerable viability and can act as rich deposit from which to develop a creative and ameliorative social philosophy.

CULTURAL PEDAGOGY: THE COMMON SOURCE OF OUR PERSONAL EXPECTATIONS, SENSIBILITIES, AND EVALUATIONS

I.

Time moves fast in America. We are a people for whom event and obsolescence are almost simultaneous. The intense and sometimes shrill critique of our institutions which rent the air of the last decade has now retreated to an eerie whisper, with only nostalgia on which to feed. We live in a culture that is suffering severe withdrawal symptoms, a culture which no longer has confidence either in its achievements or in the efficacy of its complaints. We ask, were those criticisms and protests of the last decade so far off the mark that they quickly became irrelevant or did they cut so deep that they inflicted a near-fatal wound? And again, was our earlier cynicism about institutional reform so telling that its outcome was inevitably a response of boredom to our world, to others, and even to ourselves?

In our judgment the critiques issued in the previous decade cut deep, but they need not be fatal, at least not if we face them squarely. Undoubtedly, the aesthetic and political countercultures of the last decade still have much to teach us about our present situation and, above all, about directions for our future. As with most radical movements in American history, their demise does not obviate their significance or the subtle spreading of their bequest. We offer that in at least three major areas of American cultural sensibility we have undergone a subtle but important shift in our experience and in our expectation. Specifically, we point to our attitude toward scientific progress, our experience of time, and our confidence about institutional transformation. To avoid coming to grips with these concerns is to render naive any subsequent commentary on a new cultural pedagogy. We regard the recent counterculture movements as an exacerbated symptom, an early warning system, pointing to the need for us to reconsider long-assumed styles and priorities. And if it can be said that we have experienced a heightened sensitivity to the presence of an underlying disorientation in our culture, it cannot be said that we have been able thus far to articulate adequately the cause and nature of this disorientation. Our failure to recast the nature of our expectations and our modes of inquiry, relative to the kinds of experiences we have been having, has led to deepening frustration and an erosion of energy.

Our first consideration has to do with science. We have come to distrust science as a guarantor of salvation and with the advent of this distrust, have become decidedly skeptical of the inevitability of progress. The theme of progress to which we as Americans have paid aggressive allegiance in the past once convinced us, however indirectly, that the future was to be an improvement.[2] In colloquial terms, an American was convinced that tomorrow would be better than today and if we paid dues, things would work out. The price to be paid for such improvement was rarely stated and, if known at all, was discovered only in retrospect. In the past, the assessment of our immediate situation, especially in its negative import, was diluted by the confidence we had in a healing and fruitful future.

The promise of science as the harbinger of guaranteed progress induced in us a cultural myopia, whereby we lost sight of the many implications of such progress, and in certain instances we even lost sight of the steep and perhaps catastrophic prices to be paid for such advances. The energy and ecological crises are salient examples of such myopia. Revealing, too, is the offensive gap between the achievements of American experimental medicine and the inept character of our national health-care delivery system. Yet, those who attempted to resist the lure of dramatic progress as found in the linear breakthroughs of scientific research, often applied indiscriminately, were castigated by the use of the simplistic but psychologically devastating charge of anti-intellectualism. This charge was made despite the fact that a truly intellectual position should be skeptical of any breakthrough, no matter how dramatic, when it cannot account for the relational setting from which it proceeds and for the range of effects which it is sure to have.

At this point in our history, it seems that we have become considerably apprised of the gravity of unreflective progress. Discovery does not thrill us as it once did but rather evokes in us a wariness, for we know too well that breakthroughs in one area all too often carry with them ghastly by-products, some of them timed to erupt generations hence, as witness the aberrant use of the drug thalidomide. And we are no longer necessarily impressed by the ostentatious conquest of the frontiers of knowledge if those conquests generate, sustain, condone, or are even indifferent to patterns of dehumanization elsewhere. This legitimate skepticism about the excessive claims and authority of science soon degenerated, however, into generalized attacks on intellectual research and reflective inquiry overall. At the height of the counterculture movements this attitude was reduced to the banal confrontation between relevance and irrelevance, the definitions of which remained elusive and self-serving. In some quarters the diagnosis cut deeper, amounting to nothing less than a "bleak cynicism" in response to the institutional forms of contemporary society.[3]

II.

Now, from one point of view, the emergence of a widespread cynicism should not come as a complete surprise. As the century moves into its last quarter, the long-standing confidence in eschatological redemption is at its lowest ebb. The theological promises of Christianity and the more recent sociological promises of Marxism are now more utilized as contributors to a liberated present than they are trusted to deliver a paradisiacal future. Even more modest formulations of a political and social future, such as the varieties of democracy, have shown themselves capable of massive self-deception. Searing events of recent historical memory such as the Holocaust, totalitarian labor camps, Hiroshima, Biafra, and Vietnam seem

From Cynicism to Amelioration

to lend an imprimatur to the assumption that the historical significance of life is folly and that progress is illusory. Certainly, if the meaning of progress is wedded to an assured future, then we are doomed to disappointment, traceable not only to the catastrophic events which pockmark our century but as well to that inevitable death which closes out every human life. From the point of view of a cultural pedagogy, that is, institutional efforts to enhance personal life, what troubles us here is not the necessary acknowledgement of the irreducible character of these historical facts but the reemergence of an appeal to an ancient resolution, the doctrine of the cycle. Now used as something of a speculative deus ex machina, the emphasis on patterns of cultural return and repetition is held to account for the meaning of human life in a way that is virtually independent of the development of our social, political, and institutional history. Many contemporary social and religious movements in America are characterized by this deemphasis on local intelligibility and by a withdrawal from the exigencies of social and political change. Introverted in style and concern, these movements are less counterculture than they are indifferent to the larger social webbing in which they reside. Whether they be orthodox in presentation as the Hare Krishna or more pluraslistic as in the countless versions of Zen, Yoga regimen, Tai Chi, or Meditation, they have selectively appropriated the language and themes of ancient traditions and congealed into an ahistorical response to contemporary life.

Actually, a more accurate view of the doctrine of the cycle will show that its contemporary adherents are advocating a simplistic and misleading version of what in fact is a host of complex interpretations of the fabric of reality. Surely, the ancient traditions of Buddhism and Hinduism cannot be described in the simple terms of a commitment to historical repetition. For example, despite his entitling of a major work, *The Human Cycle*, the important twentieth-century Indian thinker Sri Aurobindo has a deep sense of political evolution.[4] So too was there also a deep awareness of change and growth in the fundamental notion of Greek thought, the *apeiron*, which yields the being and becoming of all reality. Likewise can it be said of those modern Western European thinkers who focus on the theme of recurrence, such as Vico, Nietzsche, and James Joyce, that they are superbly attuned to the nuances and messagings of their respective cultures.

Nonetheless, it can be attributed to such generalized approaches to the human saga that they harbor a deep skepticism about the efficacy of building the future day by day and reveal also an aggressive distrust of the claims of novelty, so important to the practitioners of linear history. Even James Joyce, who, in all of literature, has given us perhaps the most exquisite and evocative description of our immediate experiences, repeatedly stresses the recurrence and internalization of our conscious life. The wisdom and imagination so characteristic of these cyclical versions of human life should not cloak from view that they lead to an erosion of political energy. Indeed, in reference to the more contemporary, counterculture use of these traditions, a polemic would contend that a return to the doctrine of the cycle as a principle of explanation is a rationalization on behalf of the refusal to confront the ultimate inexplicability of historical processes. In turn, this rationalization breeds a consequent justification of an abandonment of personal responsibility for the quality of our collective social and political life.

Lest the reader be unconvinced of the straight line between cyclic consciousness and severe dubiety about social and political ameliorative efforts, we cite the work of Norman O. Brown. Not to be relegated to the status of a counterculture guru, Brown offers us a biting and perceptive critique of the social and psychological assumptions of contemporary society, only to prophesy its healing by an appeal to the cycle. Beginning with *Life Against Death*,[5] Brown assaults linear history as the source of our deepest troubles. He cites with favor Stephen's comment in Joyce's *Ulysses* that "history is a nightmare from which I am trying to awake."[6] For Brown, "psychoanalysis can provide a theory of 'progress,' but only by viewing history as a neurosis."[7] The building of a civilization is the supreme act of self-deception, trapping us in a series of bad-faith flights from death. Subsequently, in an impassioned Phi Beta Kappa address in 1961, Brown points to the "way out." Reminiscent of the prophetic utterances of Emerson's address more than a century ago, but with a vastly different message, Brown elicits the source of our liberation.

And so there comes a time—I believe we are in such a time—when civilization has to be renewed by the discovery of new mysteries, by the undemocratic but sovereign power of the imagination, by the undemocratic power which makes poets the unacknowledged legislators of mankind, the power which makes all things new.

The power which makes all things new is magic. What our time needs is mystery: what our time needs is magic. Who would not say that only a miracle can save us?[8]

This text is no isolated or transient remark of Brown, for he repeats most of it in his most recent book, appropriately entitled *Closing Time*.[9] In an admittedly brilliant commentary on Vico and Joyce, Brown's theme in *Closing Time* is stated as: "First the age of the gods, then the age of heroes, then the age of men. The origin is sacred: the decline is secularization, process is profanation."[10]

In effect, Brown holds that to build a civilization is to mislead and to be misled. He contends that the deepest realization of aesthetic sensibility requires that we "drop out" from the affairs and burdens of linear time. In *Life Against Death*, he writes that a "city is itself, like money, crystallized guilt."[11] In a later essay, "From Politics to Metapolitics," Brown holds that: "Technological rationality can be put to sleep so that something else can awaken in the human mind, something like the God Dionysus, something which cannot be programmed."[12]

What, then, is this "miracle" which will save us? Brown answers: nothing less than a return to our origins, to "primitive simplicity," where we await and greet the "return of the Gods."[13] And what should we do in the meantime but witness the "return of barbarism," which signals the second, or third, or fourth coming. Perhaps Brown has a remark of Emerson in mind, "when half-gods go, the gods arrive."[14] Yet, should we ask whether, upon arrival shall the gods stay, and more importantly, whether there are gods at all? Surely these are open questions, and they press us to ask still another. What of us now? That is, in fundamental human terms, what do we do while waiting? At a minimum, in the interim, we should remind ourselves that the doctrine of the cycle is not the only bequest of antiquity relative to the meaning of history and time.

At this point in contemporary culture, we should renew awareness of an alternative approach to the meaning of history, namely, that nurtured by the Hebrew Bible and which succeeding generations of Jewish life have brought to world consciousness. No longer exclusively Jewish, and in some recent traditions, dramatically secularized, this ancient vision stresses historical lineage, prophecy with political responsibility, accrued wisdom and salvation in time upon the earth. For this tradition, the lesson of time has been that the focus should not concentrate so much on the goal as on the journey, which in turn, carries its own worth. The future stretches before us, unguaranteed, its quality for better or worse in our own hands. Chary of mysticism, secrets, false gods, cycles, and ever wary of broken promises, this vision of historical destiny made its way into the modern world. One of its most seminal reformulations occurs in the emergence of seventeenth-century Puritanism, notably, the founders of America. Ostensibly Christians, the Puritans were more so children of the Hebrew Bible, committed once again to the journey, to salvation on the land, and to the entwining of the political and religious covenant. In no way pollyanna, the Puritan attempt to found Zion in the wilderness was deeply sensitized to the travails of time, yet refused to accept a deus ex machina, whether of ideological or eschatological origin. The history of the Puritan ethos in America is a complex one, and we do not deny that its "orthodox" followers of the nineteenth century are shallow and legalistic. Unfortunately, it was a function of such subsequent emptiness that much of American thought generated a doctrine of progress minus a deep sense of tragedy. The original Puritan sensibility, however, transformed in name and language, emerged anew in the American philosophers Emerson, James, Royce, and especially Dewey. For them, as for the Puritans and the Jewish tradition, nostrum-mongerers were to be denied their seductions. Taking up against false gods, false promises, and the illusions of ultimate salvation, they did not look for a "way out" of history. To the contrary, they attempted to understand, enhance, and ameliorate the human journey, which inexorably takes place as history. When developing a cultural pedagogy, we should pay heed to the classical American philosophers who help us to avoid cynicism while simultaneously cautioning us against the seductions of ideology and final solutions.[15]

III.

Prior to turning to the qualities of a cultural pedagogy as rooted in the thought of John Dewey, we should bring to the fore the main lines of another recent critique of contemporary society, that of Herbert Marcuse. Diagnostically similar to the critique of Norman O. Brown, Marcuse's book, *Eros and Civilization*, also provides an imaginative reading of Freud's *Civilization and Its Discontents*.[16] The disagreements between Brown and Marcuse are not to be found in their critique of society, past and present, but rather with regard to the possibilities for the future. In a text that seemingly could have been written by both of them, Marcuse holds that:

...progress itself according to its explicit concept, is laden with disturbing activity, transcendence for its own sake, unhappiness, and negativity. It becomes an unavoidable question whether the negativity inherent in the principle of progress is perhaps the motive force of progress, the force that makes it possible. Or, to formulate it in another way that establishes the link to Freud: Is progress necessarily based on unhappiness and must it necessarily remain connected to unhappiness and the lack of gratification?[17]

Brown, of course, believes that progress is necessarily based on unhappiness (read repression) and that it will remain so, for that is precisely what is meant by human history as neurosis. Marcuse, more deeply committed to Marx than is Brown,[18] contends otherwise and points to the need for "revolution in the capitalist world."[19] For Brown, the way out of the cave is to move from the politics of sublimation to symbolism, that is, to the realization that our chains are "magical." They will fall from us as we come to liberated self-consciousness, a liberation effected by the confrontation with our own inevitable death and the rejection of all sublimated posturings of immortality. In his ingeniously rich "book," *Love's Body*,[20] Brown invokes selective literary instances from our cultural past on behalf of his fundamental message. "From literalism to symbolism;

the lesson of my life. The next generation needs to be told that the real fight is not the political fight, but to put an end to politics. From politics to metapolitics. From politics to poetry."[21]

On this matter, Marcuse was quite clear. The cave is a battleground, and the chains are real. Coming to liberated consciousness does not of itself guarantee the way out.

> Waking up from sleep, finding the way out of the cave is work within the cave; slow, painful work with and *against* the prisoners in the cave....There are those who do this work, who risk their lives for it—they fight the real fight, the political fight.[22]

In a subsequent attack on the apolitical wing of the counterculture, Marcuse writes what has to be a parody of Brown's positions or, at least, of the position of those who claim to be influenced by him. Marcuse stresses the need for individual liberation, which in turn is an overcoming of the bourgeois individual. "But the bourgeois individual is not overcome by simply refusing social performance by dropping out and living one's own style of life. To be sure, no revolution without individual liberation, but also no individual liberation without the liberation of society."[23] Granted, for Marcuse is right in his insistence on a "dialectic of liberation," in which the individual is conjoined with the processes of radical social change. Marcuse is not innocent of the fact that such simultaneous "liberations" have not been characteristic of previous revolutionary consciousness, to say nothing of previous revolutions. For Marcuse, the history of mankind has been a "history of domination and servitude."[24] In Marcuse's statement of the causes of this repressive history, he assumes a theme common to both Marx and Freud. However different in style or intent, they both tell us that in the most profound recesses of our consciousness we are self-deceived, and despite social appearances to the contrary, we live secondhand lives.[25] It is this interpretive context that enables Marcuse to write:

> These causes are economic-political, but since they have shaped the very instincts and needs of men, no economic and political changes will bring this historical continuum to a stop unless they are carried through by men who are physiologically and psychologically able to experience things, and each other, outside the context of violence and exploitation.[26]

This is a remarkable text, for it makes clear that nothing less than a revolution in the experience of our bodies is necessary if a genuine social and political revolution is to take place. Marcuse had written earlier that "cultural needs" can "sink down" into our instinctual life and thereby sustain, if not develop, patterns of aggression and guilt, which he takes as requisites for the maintenance of contemporary society.[27] In effect, despite his persistent calling for a "revolution in the capitalist world," Marcuse sees that such a revolution has as its linch-pin the emergence of a "new sensibility," which expresses the ascent of the life instincts over aggressiveness and guilt."[28] Perhaps we can say that at this point Marcuse brings the wisdom of Freud to bear on the pages of Marx's "Economic and Philosophical Manuscripts of 1844."[29] To Marx's brilliant analysis of alienation, Marcuse carries the message of Eros: "aesthetic needs have their own social content."[30] Marcuse is aware that revolutionary consciousness is vacant and counterproductive if it does not proceed from a genuine revolution in personal "sensibility," which, in turn, protects us from those new forms of "social immortality" so omnipresent as the backfill of classical revolutions.

> The new sensibility has become, by this very token, *praxis*: it emerges in the struggle against violence and exploitation where this struggle is waged for essentially new ways and forms of life: negation of the entire Establishment, its morality, culture, affirmation of the right to build a society in which the abolition of poverty and toil terminates in a universe where the sensuous, the playful, the calm, and the beautiful become forms of existence and thereby the *Form* of the society itself.[31]

Certainly this is a highly desirable state of affairs, which Marcuse details for our future. And we applaud Marcuse's insistence on the central importance of the new sensibility in any social and political revolution. On a closer look, however, certain difficulties do emerge from Marcuse's version of our situation. The first has to do with the distinction made by Marcuse between rebellion and revolution. In the *Essay on Liberation*, despite his praising much of the aesthetic style of the counterculture, one still had the nagging feeling that his praise was programmatic rather than genuinely enthusiastic. For Marcuse, the significance of modern art, black American music, and new forms of literature and poetry seemed to proceed more from their antiestablishment animus than from their distinctive aesthetic quality. They are to be regarded as rebellious but not as revolutionary. Put stridently, the last pages of Marcuse's chapter on "The New Sensibility" gave the impression that after the revolution, we would all listen to Beethoven. That such a judgment is not excessive finds its support in a line from Marcuse's later work, *Counterrevolution and Revolt:* "Co-option threatens the cultural revolution: ecology rock, ultramodern art are the most conspicuous examples."[32] Revolutionary consciousness turns out to be "fussy" consciousness, whereby much of the aesthetic sensibility developed in recent decades is to be regarded as merely a step on behalf of the "revolution." In the midst of Marcuse's revolutionary rhetoric, high culture rears its head and the result is condescension. Surely we can agree with Marcuse that "the most extreme political content does not repel traditional forms."[33] Such an acceptance does not mean, however, that we are limited to traditional forms, much less saddled with them. No revolutionary design is necessary to justify the aesthetic significance of the music of Charlie Parker or the painting of Jackson Pollock.

A second difficulty in Marcuse's position is that operatively it seems to contain a vicious cycle. If we accept Marcuse's judgment that the history of civilization has been repressive and has reworked even our instinctual life so as to sustain patterns of aggression and guilt, then who is to effect the revolution? As Marx before him, Marcuse contends that thus far we have not experienced genuine revolution but only rebellion. The historical result has been to replace one political facade, one bureaucratic apparatus, with another, changing rhetoric and intent without effecting genuine liberation.[34] Even given the possibility, which by Marcuse's own strictures seems unlikely, that some of a future generation would come to a liberated consciousness, conjoining sensibility, rationality, and revolutionary commitment, the following problem emerges. How could those in question sustain that consciousness through the travails of a violent revolution and the attendant decisions which arise inevitably in the reconstituting of the economic, social, and political fabric of human life? "Apparatchik" are not born; they are made by the urgency and complexity of such decisions. Is it a parody or a lamentable truth when it is said that after the revolution names change but things are the same?

By way of escaping this circle, Marcuse rests on a veiled restatement of the older Marxist eschatology,[35] that history is on our side. He opens his chapter on "The New Sensibility" by admitting that his theoretical projection would seem "to be fatally premature—were it not for the fact that the awareness of the transcendent possibilities of freedom must become a driving power in the consciousness and the imagination which prepare the soil for this revolution."[36] Marcuse's notion of transcendence is decidedly secular in that it does not reflect a world outside of time. Nonetheless, it is a force which ostensibly will take us to a new "historical stage"[37] and, as a revolution, will be "essentially different."[38] Despite its secularity, this transcendence is more an item of faith than it is of knowledge and, as a social strategy, scarcely more convincing than the invisible hand of the eighteenth-century liberals. Indeed, with regard to the transcendent possibilities spoken of by Marcuse, or for that matter, transcendence of any other stripe, why has it been so hidden, so stingy, so banal? Or perhaps we have looked in the wrong direction, for if the twentieth century is an index, transcendence reveals that we have been in the hands of a *mal génie*. As the Manicheans long ago taught us, the claim of one kind of transcendence invokes the other.

In his response to Marcuse's critique of *Love's Body*, Norman O. Brown had written, "My friend Marcuse and I: Romulus and Remus quarreling; which of them is the *real* 'revolutionary'?"[39] To the extent that either of them wishes to be so called, they are both revolutionary in their critique of existing society. They are very traditional, however, when one considers their confidence in a liberated and unified future.[40] This is a confidence which we regard as dangerously illusory, for it generates judgments about the quality of our present experiences on behalf of a future which has not yet, and may not ever, come to pass. This is not to gainsay that Brown and Marcuse are tellingly perceptive when they argue that any fundamental transformation of human society will trace to a heightening and enhancing of personal aesthetic sensibility. We caution, however, that neither the dialectic of history as bequeathed by Marx nor the chtonic energies released by Dionysus are guaranteed to save us or to protect us from the irreducible problematic of the human situation, our personal and inevitable death. Freud had referred to death as the "immortal adversary"[41] of Eros. At the close of *Life Against Death*, Brown asks if, "perhaps" our children can see in that "old adversary, a friend."[42] Perhaps. More likely, our children will see themselves in the same paradoxical situation as our own: called to ameliorate our condition by striving for saving experiences in a world apparently devoid of salvation.

Contrary to much of the commentary on American optimism and historical innocence, this stark version of our situation is a more accurate index of our reflective tradition[43] and is found as a major strand in our philosophical and literary history. The experience and articulation of alienation is a persistent theme of American poets, just as the garrulousness of our political style hides an abiding, irreducible awareness of human finitude and of the novel styles, generation by generation, of human folly and self-deception. An important question emerges here. What are the qualities of a cultural pedagogy if amelioration rather than salvation is the touchstone for evaluation and decision?

IV.

Now in an issue as important as the development of a cultural pedagogy, it will not do to state simply that one should cut between the interpretations of Brown and Marcuse, between the doctrine of the cycle and that of revolutionary consciousness. It is true that a staple of traditional American thought has been the avoidance of extremes, but we must also face the fact that in contemporary America, advocates of a centrist position are most often bereft of imagination and have displayed little moral or political courage. And

From Cynicism to Amelioration

we admit that it would be atavistic to reinvoke the thought of an earlier philosopher, John Dewey, as a solvent for present ills. Despite the incredible range of Dewey's thought, written over a seventy-year span, from the time of Darwin to that of the Korean War,[44] it is important to realize that his philosophy was not wrought out of the two catastrophic events of the mid-twentieth century, the Holocaust and the "bomb." Furthermore, Dewey's philosophy takes inadequate cognizance of our now deep awareness of personal and collective self-deception, rendered in political terms as co-optation.[45]

Nonetheless, American culture does harbor a philosophical tradition that can respond to contemporary needs if given sufficient recasting. Granted the dating of exemplifications and of some formulations, John Dewey is still the most eloquent and incisive spokesman for a distinctively American cultural pedagogy. We focus here on Dewey's notion of aesthetic experience and its pedagogical significance for our efforts to ameliorate human institutions. We assume as a historical context for this discussion a generalized statement of the notion of experience characteristic of American culture and a radically empirical doctrine of relations, both themes I have treated elsewhere.[46]

At the beginning of his philosophical career, Dewey was a Hegelian. Primarily due to the influence of William James's *Principles of Psychology*, published in 1890, Dewey began to develop his own philosophy of experience. Whether the concern was psychological, epistemological, or educational, the theme of experience became increasingly central, as witness, selectively, "The Reflex Arc Concept in Psychology" (1896), "The Postulate of Immediate Empiricism" (1905), and *Democracy and Education* (1916).[47] In 1917, Dewey wrote an essay on "The Need for a Recovery of Philosophy," which contrasted the orthodox description of experience with what he held to be more "congenial to present conditions." In that contrast, Dewey's version of experience stressed its experimental character, connection with a future, inferentiality, and affectivity. For Dewey, experience is "an affair of the intercourse of a living being with its physical and social environment." Further, "an experience that is an undergoing of an environment and a striving for its control in new directions is pregnant with connections."⁴⁸ The physicality, if not sexuality, of Dewey's language should not be overlooked in the present discussion. Lacking the flamboyance of both Brown and Marcuse, Dewey nonetheless is setting the stage for a philosophy of culture in which the activity of the body is the prime analogate for evaluations of social and political life.

In 1925, Dewey published *Experience and Nature*,⁴⁹ which gives to his notion of experience its major formulation. Cast as a metaphysics, the book is also a philosophy of culture, as Dewey himself acknowledged in subsequent reflection. While preparing a new, and never-to-appear, edition of *Experience and Nature* in 1951, Dewey decided to change the title to "Nature and Culture." At that time, he wrote, "I was dumb not to have seen the need for such a shift when the old text was written. I was still hopeful that the [philosophic] word 'experience' would be redeemed by [being] returned to its idiomatic usages—which was a piece of historic folly, the hope, I mean...."⁵⁰ In his first chapter, "Experience and Philosophic Method," Dewey sets out his fundamental position that "experience is *of* as well as *in* nature."⁵¹ He details this judgment in the following way:

> It is not experience which is experienced, but nature—stones, plants, animals, diseases, health, temperature, electricity, and so on. Things interacting in certain ways *are* experience; they are what is experienced. Linked in certain other ways with another natural object—the human organism—they are *how* things are experienced as well. Experience thus reaches down into nature; it has depth. It also has breadth and to an indefinitely elastic extent. It stretches. That stretch constitutes inference.⁵²

Although telescoped in style, this text indicates Dewey's understanding of our fundamental situation, and it provides the basis for his integration of the multiple reflective approaches which constitute a philosophy of culture. The setting is the transaction⁵³ of the human organism with nature or with the environment. Nature has a life of its own, undergoing its own relatings, which in turn become what we experience. Our own transaction with the affairs of nature cuts across the givenness of nature and our ways of relating. This is *how* we experience *what* we experience. Dewey was a realist in the sense that the world exists independent of our thought of it, but the

From Cynicism to Amelioration

meaning *of* the world is inseparable from our *meaning* the world. Experience, therefore, is not headless, for it teems with relational leads, inferences, implications, comparisons, retrospections, directions, warnings, and so on. The rhythm of *how* we experience is an aesthetic, having as its major characteristic the relationship between anticipation and consummation, yet having other perturbations, as mishap, loss, boredom, and listlessness. Pedagogy becomes, then, the twin effort to integrate the directions of experience with the total needs of the person and to cultivate the ability of an individual to generate new potentialities in his experiencing and to make new relationships so as to foster patterns of growth. And politics is the struggle to construct an optimum environment for the realizing and sanctioning of the aesthetic processes of living. Finally, the entire human endeavor should be an effort to apply the method of creative intelligence in order to achieve optimum possibilities in the never-ending moral struggle to harmonize the means-end relationship[54] for the purpose of enhancing human life and achieving growth. Dewey sees this effort as central to a philosophy of culture. In a chapter significantly entitled "The Construction of Good," he describes our "deepest problem."

> The problem of restoring integration and cooperation between man's beliefs about the world in which he lives and his beliefs about the values and purposes that should direct his conduct is the deepest problem of modern life. It is the problem of any philosophy that is not isolated from that life.[55]

The beliefs of which Dewey speaks are not foreordained, only to be uncovered by sagacious announcement. They emerge from the struggles of the human organism in its attempt to understand and ameliorate its condition by virtue of *experimental* inquiry. Some might say that Dewey's description of our "deepest problem" is prosaic, for terms such as "integration," "cooperation," "values," and "purposes" are hardly the stuff of highly charged social and political movements. Precisely, for Dewey is describing our "ordinary" experience, which he considers to be a far more accurate description of actual situation than those tantalizing but misleading rhetorical formulations of variant salvation myths. For Dewey, the world is intelligible, although not ultimately so, and thereby his fundamental attitude is neither pessimistic nor optimistic. In the tradition of Emerson, Lester Frank Ward, and William James, Dewey is a meliorist. In contrast to assorted prophets and more strident claimants of social and political vision, Dewey promises little and delivers much. And finally, long before recent counterculture movements, Dewey was aware that a heightening of aesthetic experience was of essential importance to *any* form of liberation.

We must admit, however, that Dewey is rarely read this way. To some extent, he is to blame for generating misunderstandings of his position.[56] It is especially unfortunate that he did not integrate sufficiently his aesthetics with his political writings. This gap was exacerbated in his social and political writings of the 1930s, in which he utilized the language of social planning as his way of responding to the competing Marxist and laissez-faire formulations of that time. It is instructive that this period is also represented by publication of his profound work in aesthetics, *Art as Experience*, in 1934. This work comes at a midpoint between his major writings in social and political philosophy: *The Public and Its Problems* (1927), *Individualism Old and New* (1930), *Liberalism and Social Action* (1935), and *Freedom and Culture* (1939). For our purposes, it will be best to concentrate on the last chapter of *Liberalism and Social Action*, which Dewey titles "Renascent Liberalism" and which is the clearest statement of his politics. We can then bring to bear upon that discussion some of his views about the importance of aesthetic experience.

In "Renascent Liberalism," Dewey takes a position which is clearly counter to that held by Brown or by Marcuse, and actually, if we were not anachronistic, we could say that he had them in mind. The chapter begins with Dewey sorting out three obvious interpretive approaches to social and political change. The first is that change does not or should not take place. If it does take place, it is due to a preordained plan, or at a minimum, such change is of no affair of ours, tracing to forces operative elsewhere. This is a veiled reference to laissez-faire liberalism or to its later version in social Darwinism. Dewey regards this position as naive, reflecting as it does that "men's minds are still pathetically held in the clutch of old habits and haunted by old memories."[57] Lamentably, he does not focus on the fact that this position is most often taken by those who have most to benefit by the absence of radical change, especially that brought about by revolutionary intervention.

The second position is that significant change can take place only by means of violence. Dewey traces this propensity for radical solution to deep insecurity based on a long-standing human experience of scarcity. Then, in a text worthy of Marx, Dewey points to the presence of a dramatic difference in an industrial culture.

> The conditions that generate insecurity for the many no longer spring from nature. They are found in institutions and arrangements that are within deliberate human control. Surely this change marks one of the greatest revolutions that has taken place in all human history. Because of it, insecurity is not now the motive to work and sacrifice but to despair.[58]

Finally, Dewey offers his own version, which is to acknowledge the inexorability of change, while setting our task as one of directing it by the utilization of social intelligence. The backdrop to this position was written earlier by Dewey in *The Public and Its Problems*. "The creation of a *tabula rasa* in order to permit the creation of a new order is so impossible as to set at naught both the hope of buoyant revolutionaries and the timidity of scared conservatives."[59] Dewey contends that education holds the key to liberation, especially if it develops programs of action for fundamental institutional reform. He is skeptical of the significance of sheerly personal patterns of liberation if they do not coalesce to effect substantial changes in our social and political beliefs, for "the educational task cannot be accomplished merely by working on men's minds, without action that effects actual change in institutions."[60]

Lest the reader think that Dewey was innocent of the obstacles to such institutional change, we cite his statement of 1928: "The notion that men are equally free to act irrespective of differences in education, in command of capital, and the control of the social environment which is furnished by the institution of property—is a pure absurdity, as facts have demonstrated."[61]

And he returns to this theme in "Renascent Liberalism," where he again points to the coercive power flowing from the ownership of property. "It is foolish to regard the political state as the only agency now endowed with coercive power. Its exercise of this power is pale in contrast with that exercised by concentrated and organized property interests."[62] Despite his admission of the coercive power arrayed against the possibilities of liberation, Dewey warns that to accept the inevitability of our present situation is to allow for violence as the only means of effective change. Further, the "reign of the inevitable" prevents the use of intelligence, which in Dewey's judgment should be experimental, innovative, and constructive. We do not stand outside of our institutions as hapless observers, nor are we trapped in a historical past that rigidly programs our present. Each historical context demands its own evaluation and its own strategies for effective transformation. "The radical who insists that the future method of change must be like that of the past has much in common with the hide-bound reactionary who holds to the past as an ultimate fact. Both overlook the *fact that history in being a process of change generates change not only in details but also in the method of directing social change.*"[63]

Dewey then indicates here and in other of his political writings that the decisively new factor in the twentieth century is the availability of an experimental method of intelligence, reflective of the cooperative approach found in the natural sciences. He does not relate this method explicitly at this point to his understanding of the method of experience as found in his pedagogy, nor to his notion of aesthetic experience, although in "Renascent Liberalism" he writes of the need for an "embodiment of intelligence" if we are to "know where to turn for the means of directing further change."[64] Given the events of the last two decades, it would be fair to question Dewey's confidence in science as the exemplary method for the development of social intelligence. On the other hand, he was prescient in his emphasis on aesthetic sensibility as central to a liberated human life. Indeed, Dewey's understanding of experience as aesthetic may turn out to be more politically significant than his explicitly political writings.

We do not attempt here to show the relevance of Dewey's aesthetics to concrete social and cultural issues, choosing rather in the context of our discussion of Brown and Marcuse to sketch Dewey's assessment of the kind of sensibility most fruitful for human life. He stands with Emerson, for whom "every ingenious and aspiring soul leaves the doctrine behind him in his own experience...."[65] And with James, for whom "experience, as we know, has ways of *boiling over*, and making us correct our present formulas."[66] In Dewey's philosophy experience is undergone in the transaction of the human organism with nature, a transaction which is clearly an "embodiment." The human existential situation yields generic traits, and for Dewey, the most fundamental are the "stable" and the "precarious." These traits do not divide the world, nor are entities or situations simply one or the other. They are not divisions between self and world, between you and me, between yesterday and today, this and that. Rather, the precarious and the stable live as irreducible entwinings in every event. In Buberian terms, their relationship constitutes our melancholy fate. Make no mistake, ameliorative politics notwithstanding, Dewey's description of our world is not always cheering.

> A feature of existence which is emphasized by cultural phenomena is the precarious and the perilous....Time is brief, and this statement must stand instead of the discourse which the subject deserves. Man finds himself living in an aleatory world; his existence involves, to put it baldly, a gamble. The world is a scene of risk; it is uncertain, unstable, uncannily unstable. Its dangers are irregular, inconstant, not to be counted upon as to their times and seasons. Although persistent, they are sporadic, episodic. It is darkest just before dawn; pride goes before a fall; the moment of greatest prosperity is the moment most charged with ill-omen, most opportune for the evil eye. Plague, famine, failure of crops, disease, death, defeat in battle, are always just around the corner, and so are abundance, strength, victory, festival and song. Luck is proverbially both good and bad in its distributions. The sacred and the accursed are potentialities of the same situation; and there is no category of things which has not embodied the sacred and accursed: persons, words, places, times, directions in space, stones, winds, animals, stars.[67]

The alternating rhythm of the precarious and the stable is also the alternating rhythm of our "embodiment" in nature, yielding the penalties and possibilities of temporality. Each of us has his own rhythm, his own needs. Our experiences move from the inchoate to the consummatory, a journey striated with blocked expectations, surprises, bypasses, and periodic realizations. Dewey urges us to live our lives on the *qui vive,* always alert to our surroundings as if with animal sensibility. The most perilous threat to human life is secondhandedness, living out the bequest of our parents, siblings, relatives, teachers, and other dispensers of already programmed possibilities. We should be wary of the inherited, however noble its intention, for it is the quality of our own experience which is decisive. Failure, deeply undergone, often enriches, whereas success achieved mechanically through the paths set out by others often blunts sensibility. We are not dropped into the world as a thing among things. We are live creatures who eat experience.

No creature lives merely under its skin; its subcutaneous organs are means of connection with what lies beyond its bodily frame, and to which, in order to live, it must adjust itself, by accommodation and defense but also by conquest. At every moment, the living creature is exposed to dangers from its surroundings, and at every moment, it must draw upon something in its surroundings to satisfy its needs. The career and destiny of a living being are bound up with its interchanges with its environment, not externally but in the most intimate way.[68]

The signal achievement of Dewey's approach is that he has shifted the source of evaluation for human life from "what" to "how." Stated otherwise, Dewey is not sanguine about any final resolution to the human condition, especially if it is presented in the form of an all-solving panacea, be it religious or political. He does, however, believe that the human condition, despite its insoluble and perilous character, can be tremendously enhanced if we learn to assess, celebrate, and sanction the ways in which we undergo our ordinary experience. "How" we experience becomes more of an index to the quality of our life than "what" we experience. Has Brown or Marcuse written anything quite so revolutionary as that? Despite their radical stance on behalf of personal liberation, would they subscribe to either of the following texts from Dewey?

a. An experience, a very humble experience, is capable of generating and carrying any amount of theory (or intellectual content), but a theory apart from an experience cannot be definitely grasped even as a theory.[69]

b. Even a crude experience, if authentically an experience is more fit to give a clue to the intrinsic nature of esthetic experience than is an object already set apart from any other mode of experience.[70]

I think not. Yet Dewey anticipates Brown and Marcuse in sensing that our real enemies are those who destroy aesthetic sensibility, whether they proceed from excessive authority, condescension, or indifference. In a jeremiad stylistically worthy of Cotton Mather, Dewey warns us against the humdrum, slackness, submission to convention, tightness, rigid abstinence, coerced submission, dissipation, incoherence, and aimless indulgence.[71] A genuinely liberated social and political environment is one which encourages the individual, who is, after all, not ready-made[72] to experience the world in all of its potential intensity. Such a situation does not protect us from the aforementioned generic trait of the precarious from which Dewey believes there to be no final escape. In certain situations the precarious is the source of our terror, whereas in other situations it is the source of our growth. To build a world is to turn the precarious to our advantage, knowing all the while that in some form it shall be with us to the end. Although our endless struggle with the precarious may be an index to an imperfect world, it is also the occasion of our distinctively human celebrations. In Dewey's language, to undergo the experience of the world as precarious is to suffer. It is arrogant to state that suffering is a necessary ingredient for a life of celebration. Yet, who among us has lived a profound, creative, and aesthetically rich life, knowing only the stable? In Dewey's judgment, the basis of a cultural pedagogy is not to be found in a transcendent force, nor in the abandonment of our historical burdens. It is to be found close-up, in the message of our bodies.

Life itself consists of phases in which the organism falls out of step with the march of surrounding things and then recovers unison with it—either through effort or by some happy chance. And, in a growing life, the recovery is never mere return to a prior state, for it is enriched by the state of disparity and resistance through which it has successfully passed. If the gap between organism and environment is too wide, the creature dies. If its activity is not enhanced by the temporary alienation, it merely subsists. Life grows when a temporary falling out is a transition to a more extensive balance of the energies of the organism with those of the conditions under which it lives.[73]

At first glance this text may appear gentle and comforting. A closer look, however, reveals that alienation and death present themselves in the course of events, and the line between the *temporary* alienation necessary to the enhancement of life and the gap of *permanent* alienation which spells death, physical or spiritual, is a thin one. The blame for crossing it is placed not on nature, nor on civilization, nor on a deus ex machina, but on ourselves. In John Dewey's philosophy, the task of overcoming personal and social alienation and reconstituting the processes of living within the flow of time is one which is laced with chance, happy and otherwise, but the responsibility is ours and ours alone.

NOTES

1. William James, *Pragmatism* (Cambridge, Mass.: Harvard University Press, 1975), p. 30.

2. From the vast literature about the notion of progress in American thought, we suggest David W. Marcell, *Progress and Pragmatism, James, Dewey, Beard and the American Idea of Progress* (Westport: Greenwood Press, 1974).

3. Theodore Roszak, *Where the Wasteland Ends* (New York: Anchor Books, 1973), passim.

4. Cf. Eugene Fontinell, "A Pragmatic Approach to the Human Cycle," *Six Pillars*, ed. Robert A. McDermott (Chambersburg: Wilson Books, 1974), pp. 129-159.

5. Norman O. Brown, *Life Against Death* (Middletown: Wesleyan University Press, 1959).

6. James Joyce, *Ulysses* (New York: Vintage Books, 1961), p. 34 (1934 edition, p. 35).

7. Brown, op. cit., p. 18.

8. Norman O. Brown, "Apocalypse: The Place of Mystery in the Life of the Mind," *Harper's Magazine*, vol. 222 (May 1961), p. 48.

9. Norman O. Brown, *Closing Time* (New York: Random House, 1973), p. 30.

10. Ibid., p. 30.

11. Ibid., p. 283.

12. Norman O. Brown, "From Politics to Metapolitics," *Caterpillar*, vol. 1 (October 1967), p. 80.

13. Brown, *Closing Time*, pp. 24, 25, 41, 63.

14. Ralph Waldo Emerson, "Give All to Love," *Works*, vol. IX (Boston: Houghton Mifflin and Co., 1904), p. 92.

15. Ernest Becker is one of the few thinkers steeped in Brown and other psychoanalytically oriented critics of contemporary society who brings to bear the American temper in his analysis. Cf. especially his posthumous book *Escape from Evil* (New York: The Free Press, 1975).

16. Cf. Herbert Marcuse, *Eros and Civilization* (Boston: The Beacon Press, 1955), and Sigmund Freud, *Civilization and Its Discontents* (London: The Hogarth Press, 1930).

17. Herbert Marcuse, "Progress and Freud's Theory of Instincts," *Five Lectures* (Boston: The Beacon Press, 1970), p. 32.

18. Cf. Norman O. Brown, "A Reply to Herbert Marcuse," in Herbert Marcuse, *Negations* (Boston: Beacon Press, 1968), p. 243. "The idea of progress is in question: the reality of Marx cannot hide the reality of Nietzsche."

19. Herbert Marcuse, *An Essay on Liberation* (Boston: The Beacon Press, 1969), p. 23.

20. Norman O. Brown, *Love's Body* (New York: Random House, 1966).

21. Brown, "Reply," p. 246.

22. Herbert Marcuse, "Love Mystified: A Critique of Norman O. Brown," *Negations*, p. 243.

23. Herbert Marcuse, *Counterrevolution and Revolt* (Boston: The Beacon Press, 1972), p. 48.

24. Marcuse, *Liberation*, p. 25.

25. As a brief textual support of this judgment, we link the following two well-known texts from Marx and Freud.

> a. The mode of production of material life conditions the social-political and intellectual life process in general. It is not the consciousness of men that determines their being, but, on the contrary, their social being that determines their consciousness. (*A Contribution to the Critique of Political Economy*, 1859).
>
> b. It is no wonder if, under the pressure of these possibilities of suffering, (from our own body, from the outer world, from our relations with other men) humanity is wont to reduce its demands for happiness, just as even the pleasure-principle itself changes into the more accommodating reality-principle under the influence of external environment; if a man thinks himself happy if he has merely escaped unhappiness or weathered trouble; if in general the task of avoiding pain forces that of obtaining pleasure into the background. (*Civilization and Its Discontents*, 1930.)

26. Marcuse, *Liberation*, p. 25.
27. Ibid., p. 10n, pp. 10–11.
28. Ibid., p. 23.
29. Cf. T.B. Bottomore, ed., *Karl Marx—Early Writings* (New York: McGraw–Hill Book Co., 1964), pp. 61–219.
30. Marcuse, *Liberation*, p. 27.
31. Ibid., p. 25. Marcuse was not always so optimistic. Cf. *Eros and Civilization*, p. 237: "But even the ultimate advent of freedom cannot redeem those who died in pain. It is the remembrance of them, and the accumulated guilt of mankind against its victims, that darken the prospect of a civilization without repression."
32. Marcuse, *Counterrevolution*, p. 49.
33. Ibid., p. 128. And we support also Marcuse's incisive critique of the anti-intellectualism generated by self-styled "revolutionaries" and vicarious participants in "proletarian ideology" (pp. 126–27).
34. Contemporary China might become an exception to this otherwise accurate judgment.
35. Marcuse, Foreword, *Negations*, p. xix. "It can be seen that precisely the most exaggerated 'eschatological' conceptions of Marxian theory most adequately anticipate social tendencies: for instance, the idea of the abolition of labor, which Marx himself later rejected." This is vintage historical eschatology, for it warns even the prophet against changing his mind.
36. Marcuse, *Liberation*, p. 23.
37. Cf. Herbert Marcuse, *Reason and Revolution* (Boston: The Beacon Press, 1960) (1941), p. 315. "Truth, in short, is not a realm apart from historical reality, nor a region of eternally valid ideas. To be sure, it transcends the given historical reality, but only in so far as it crosses from one historical stage to another."
38. Marcuse, *Liberation*, p. 23.
39. Brown, "Reply," p. 243.
40. Marcuse, *Eros*, p. 236. "The necessity of death does not refute the possibility of final liberation." And Brown closes *Closing Time* with the belief, "here comes everybody" on "the way to the unification of the human race" (p. 109).
41. Freud, *Civilization*, p. 144.
42. Brown, *Life*, p. 322.
43. It is striking that Marcuse, a man of considerable learning in the history of philosophy, literature and the arts, has never integrated American cultural history into his aggressive and even hostile version of American society. From Marcuse, we have virtually no response to Melville, Whitman, William James, Dewey, Royce, Faulkner, and countless others whose writings reveal both the wisdom and malevolence of America. Certainly Marcuse does

not breed confidence in his critique of American society when, in the face of an extensive interpretive literature, he makes slurring remarks about Puritanism as though that term still had only the ambience of sustaining the repression of the body (*Negations*, p. 265; *Liberation*, p. 28). Finally, if self-posturing and self-deception as to the meaning of "doing good" really do constitute the Achilles' heel of America, then nothing Marcuse has written is as incisively critical as Herman Melville's classic, *The Confidence Man*.

44. For a selection of Dewey's writings which show the wide range of his concerns, cf. John J. McDermott, ed., *The Philosophy of John Dewey*, 2 vols. (New York: G.P. Putnam's Sons, 1973).

45. Unfortunately, Dewey responded more to the programmatic suggestions of the Marxists than to the thought of Marx himself, and, incredibly, he never wrote a serious study of the implications of the thought of Freud.

46. "An American Notion of Experience" and "Life Is in the Transitions," *The Culture of Experience* (New York: New York University Press, 1976), pp. 1-20, 99-117.

47. For a critical edition of the writings of Dewey published before 1899, cf. *The Early Works, 1882-1898*, 5 vols. (Carbondale: Southern Illinois University Press, 1969-1972). *The Middle Works, 1899-1924*, are in process of publication, vols. 7 and 8 (Carbondale: Southern Illinois University Press, 1979).

48. John Dewey, "The Need for a Recovery of Philosophy," in McDermott, *The Philosophy of John Dewey*, p. 61.

49. John Dewey, *Experience and Nature* (La Salle: Open Court, 1929) (1925).

50. Sidney Ratner et al., *John Dewey and Arthur F. Bentley, A Philosophical Correspondence—1932-1951* (New Brunswick: Rutgers University Press, 1964), p. 543.

51. Dewey, *Experience and Nature*, 2d ed., p. 4.

52. Ibid., p. 4.

53. Toward the end of his life, Dewey came to prefer "transaction" over "interaction" as his basic mediating term. Cf. S. Ratner, op. cit., pp. 613-14.

54. John Dewey, *Reconstruction in Philosophy* (Boston: Beason Press, 1948) (1920), p. 73. "When we take means for ends we indeed fall into moral materialism. But when we take ends without regard to means we degenerate into sentimentalism. In the name of ideal we fall back upon mere luck and chance and magic or exhortation and preaching; or else upon a fanaticism that will force the realization of preconceived ends at any cost."

55. John Dewey, *The Quest for Certainty* (New York: Capricorn Books, (1960) (1929), p. 255.

56. No thinker so chary of ideology has been subjected to such intense and extreme criticism. Dewey has been accused of lowering educational

standards, threatening American ideals, having Communist sympathies, and fostering Nazism. The latest critique reports its authors standing on the Chicago River, "alienated and nauseous," holding Dewey indirectly responsible for the Vietnam War. Historically anachronistic, this essay makes Dewey a scapegoat for much that is wrong in contemporary American society. Cf. Walter Feinberg and Henry Rosemont, Jr., "Training for the Welfare State: The Progressive Education Movement." *Work, Technology and Education* (Urbana: University of Illinois Press, 1975), pp. 60–91.

57. John Dewey, *Liberalism and Social Action* (New York: Capricorn Books, 1963) (1935), p. 59.

58. Ibid., p. 60.

59. John Dewey, *The Public and Its Problems* (New York: Henry Holt and Co., 1927), p. 162.

60. Dewey, *Liberalism*, p. 61.

61. John Dewey, "Philosophies of Freedom," *Philosophy and Civilization* (New York: G.P. Putnam's Sons, 1931), p. 281. Significantly, Dewey sees the classic capitalist ethic as blocking the ameliorative possibilities of science and technology. "The greatest obstacle to that vision is, I repeat, the perpetuation of the older individualism now reduced, as I have said, to the utilization of science and technology for ends of private pecuniary gain. I sometimes wonder if those who are conscious of present ills but who direct their blows of criticism at everything except this obstacle are not stirred by motives which they unconsciously prefer to keep below consciousness." *Individualism—Old and New* (New York: G.P. Putnam's Sons, 1930), pp. 99–100.

62. Dewey, *Liberalism*, p. 64. For a recent political analysis "in the tradition of John Dewey," cf. Peter T. Manicas, *The Death of the State* (New York: G.P. Putnam's Sons, 1974).

63. Dewey, *Liberalism*, p. 83.

64. Ibid., p. 74.

65. Emerson, "Compensation." *Works*, II, 95.

66. Op. cit., p. 106.

67. Dewey, *Experience and Nature*, p. 38.

68. John Dewey, *Art as Experience* (New York: Capricorn Books, 1958) (1934), p. 13. There is historical sensibility here as well, for on page 18 Dewey writes that "the live creature adopts its past; it can make friends with even its stupidities, using them as warnings that increase present wariness."

69. John Dewey, *Democracy and Education* (New York: The Macmillan Company, 1961) (1916), p. 144.

70. Dewey, *Art as Experience*, p. 11.

71. Cf. Ibid., p. 40.

72. John Dewey, "Time and Individuality," *Time and Its Mysteries*, ed., Harlow Shapley (New York: Collier Books, 1962) (1940), p. 158.

73. Dewey, *Art as Experience*, p. 14.

PHILOSOPHY AND MORAL VALUES:
THE PRAGMATIC ANALYSIS

JAMES GOUINLOCK

WHILE MANY PHILOSOPHERS HAVE ASSUMED THAT OUR DISCIPLINE is omnicompetent in the domain of moral theory, many others have left the field altogether in the conviction that they are maintaining the purity of their enterprise. Yet there are few analyses addressed directly to the question of the competence of philosophy, as such, to deal with moral issues.

Although the question is seldom taken up specifically, I believe the inquiry would yield valuable results. We might clarify our notions about the proper concerns of philosophical ethics, and we might develop conceptions in terms of which we could determine when the vices of philosophy were those of excess or defect. It would be a broad inquiry, and if done thoroughly would have to be approached by analyzing the various features which constitute moral issues, considering each in order to see what philosophy might have to do with it. The question appears most formidable when we acknowledge that such concepts as 'philosophy,' 'morality,' 'ethics,' and 'moral theory' are indeterminate. Yet if we regard our work as intellectually respectable, we must hope for conclusions which would be congenial to diverse philosophical traditions. Deliberate investigation will at least challenge rigid habits of thought and isolate issues worthy of further attention.

I will try here to make a beginning to this inquiry by examining what I take to be the position of pragmatism in respect to it. I propose, first, to formulate a pragmatic position concerning the competence of philosophy in moral theory; second—consistently with that formulation—to indicate some of the main contributions that pragmatists have made in identifying and elucidating our moral predicaments; and, third, to comment on the continuing pertinence of the pragmatic analysis.

The treatment of such a complex subject must be selective, and the first problem of selection is obvious: there is no such animal as *the* pragmatic moral philosophy. Although there are important conceptions shared, for example, by James, Dewey, and Lewis, the respective positions of these three are by no means wholly reconcilable. There is no reason to believe that there would be a consensus in their assumptions regarding the competence of philosophy in moral theory. Accordingly, I must make some hasty decisions to bring my topic into manageable focus.

Peirce is the easiest to sacrifice in this context. He contributed little to the ethical field. His fragments suggest, moreover, that had he done so, his direction would be notably different from that taken by succeeding pragmatists. James, too, did little systematic work on the subject, although all of his writings are informed with the keenest interest in all facets of the human condition. Certainly James's peculiar form of individualism would have led him to conclusions at variance with those of Mead, Dewey, and Lewis. (I refer to James's voluntaristic ethics of belief, which he explicitly extends to moral issues.[1]) Mead also wrote regrettably little on moral philosophy, but it is safe to conclude from several of his passages that there would be no significant divergence between himself and Dewey. It is the latter, of course, who was fundamentally and persistently occupied with moral philosophy and published voluminously on most aspects of it.

In my reading of C. I. Lewis, I find that he shares many concerns in moral thought with Mead and Dewey, but his methods and conclusions are in crucial ways incompatible with theirs. Unlike them, he evidently believed it possible to establish true and invariant first principles of ethics;[2] and he did not recognize as they did the social dimensions of moral deliberation. I believe, indeed, that in a most subtle way Lewis represents one of the approaches to moral philosophy which Mead and Dewey were resisting.

Unable to survey all these thinkers, I will focus primarily, but not exclusively, on the one who devoted himself most extensively to moral thought, John Dewey. He is rightly regarded as most representative of American moral philosophy.

Philosophy and Moral Values

I.

What, according to Dewey, is the competence of the moral philosopher? It will be helpful at the outset to state Dewey's position regarding the subject matter of moral theory. Like James and Mead, he was closely identified with the actual needs and aspirations of human beings. He recognized that individuals are engaged, according to their rights, in the task of enriching the quality of their experience; and he was keenly aware that these individuals are vested with an array of moral commitments which are operative in the circumstances of life experience. This generic concern with the values implicated in all phases of experience Dewey signified with the term 'moral,' and it is to this full breadth of values that his moral philosophy is addressed.[3] He was identified with these values, not mindlessly to accept and praise them, but to help provide the knowledge and methods by which persons could criticize their varied interests and make them more inclusive, more secure and enduring. Whatever else a moral philosopher may do, he at least intends to determine the instrumentalities of thought and conduct that have the most significant bearing on the quality of life.

As a further preliminary to defining the competence of philosophy, we must overcome a regrettable stereotype. Dewey is normally called a naturalist. He actively consented to that description, and he repeatedly urged that ethics be made (in some sense) scientific. It is not surprising, then, that G. E. Moore's definition of ethical naturalism has been thought to apply to him. Accordingly, it is assumed that the core of Dewey's ethical theory consisted in the scientific definition of evaluative terms, thereby making statements with such terms in them empirically verifiable. All moral questions could be settled simply by classifying the projected outcomes of situations in accordance with the antecedent definitions.

Careful readers of Dewey will recognize that such an analysis is remote from the truth. It is belied simply in his horror of absolutism and his love of democracy. In contrast to the superficial but popular characterization, Dewey's actual conviction was that moral disagreement is an ineliminable feature of human experience. He repeatedly argued that valuations *as such* are not cognitions and therefore are not true or false. Hence, in the final analysis, they cannot be reconciled like cognitive claims. His article "Philosophy" in *The Encyclopaedia of the Social Sciences*[4] is remarkable for its emphasis on the inevitability of valuational conflicts. He argued that it is beyond the competence of philosophy to specify a moral basis for their eradication. He insisted as well that philosophers cannot prescribe moral choice. In the *Ethics*, Dewey writes,

> The difference between customary and reflective morality is precisely that definite precepts, rules, definitive injunctions and prohibitions issue from the former, while they cannot proceed from the latter.... [Moral theory] does not offer a table of commandments in a catechism in which answers are as definite are as the questions which are asked. It can render personal choice more intelligent, but it cannot take the place of personal decision, which must be made in every case of moral perplexity.[5]

In the same volume he describes his theory as democratic,[6] making it clear that he does not pretend to possession of an infallible criterion; and he elsewhere states, "The keynote of democracy as a way of life may be expressed, it seems to me, as the necessity for the participation of every mature human being in formation of the values that regulate the living of men together...."[7] "The values that regulate the living of men together" are, of course, moral values. That is, democracy is the method of the formation of moral values.

Dewey's moral theory clearly issues in the advocacy of democracy as the method for dealing with the moral problems that actually beset human conduct. He frequently refers to this method as social intelligence. Social intelligence recognizes the reality of conscientious moral conflict; it is precisely a way of dealing with such conflict. Dewey's advocacy of social intelligence is a proposal, a recommendation. He does not deduce it from first principles or present it as an unconditional imperative. He offers it as an object of choice, convinced that its adoption will go further towards fulfilling actual human needs and aspirations than any other moral method yet conceived.

Philosophy and Moral Values

Dewey believed that social intelligence is the most promising means for individuals to criticize, liberate, and fulfill their interests. He conceived it as an instrument to be put at the disposal of human beings for them to deal as effectively as possible with their typical predicaments. The manner in which Dewey proposes social intelligence suggests what to him were the aims and limits of moral philosophy; The philosopher can be a most effective *participant* in examining and clarifying moral perplexities and in enlightening our moral struggles, but cannot prescribe solutions to them. He can be most helpful; perhaps a leader, but not a lawgiver. In the next section I will return to the discussion of democracy as moral method. My topic right now is still that of determining what philosophy can do in the moral domain.

One of the best means for understanding a philosopher is to identify the problems with which he was principally concerned. It is legendary that Dewey was occupied with the putative dualisms of man and nature as conceived in modern philosophy. Why was he concerned? The reason is fundamentally a moral one: It was not primarily because these dualistic conceptions were simply mistaken, but because adherence to them obscured the urgent and perennial human effort to achieve a more welcome and satisfying experience. Modern philosophers had regarded human nature and physical nature as essentially independent systems—utterly distinct substances. Physical nature was nothing but matter in motion, and the arena of human values was relegated either to the private and subjective or to the transcendent. Conceived as subjective, experience could furnish no clue about the continuities of natural processes. The alleged realm of changeless perfection likewise gives no direction in discriminating the connections and potentialities of natural events. On such assumptions, philosophers could not in their own terms explain, much less enlighten, the processes of thought and conduct which are directed to enriching human existence in the real world.

Dewey intended, therefore, to show that these dualisms are the product of erroneous assumptions. If the dualisms can be shown to be illusory, the way is open to identifying and clarifying the instrumentalities of conduct. Our knowledge of the conjoint processes of organisms and environment would permit us to construct a more satisfactory experience. We would know how to discern and realize more values in human conduct. In conjunction with pragmatists, as well as other colleagues, he set himself to such imposing tasks as clarifying the nature of experimental intelligence, explicating the continuities of man and nature, analyzing the condition of man as a social being, characterizing the nature and sources of moral experience, and elucidating the principal traits of nature.

The pragmatists participated in these tasks in various ways, and all of them contributed to the first one mentioned. They were united in showing that ideas are means of creative activity: ideas are not summaries of sensations or copies of the antecedent structure of reality. They are predictions of future experiences that are contingent upon definite reconstructions of the present. Ideas are thus recognized as instruments of deliberate redirection of life experience; they specify the reconstructions of activity upon which the institution of valued events depends. Hence the nature of intelligent conduct is no longer obscure. Just in elucidating the continuities of thought and conduct, pragmatism contributed an invaluable advance in human self-understanding.

James and Dewey are liberating in showing that experience is the avenue to knowledge of nature, rather than a subjective barrier. In the case of Mead and Dewey, the development of the theory of the biological-social formation of human nature took on enormous import for the moral life. The conditions of the growth and enrichment of human nature were removed from the sanctuary of the allegedly individual soul and placed in the full context of culture. Mead as much as Dewey argued that we must conceive ourselves as social beings if we are to clarify the alternative aims and possibilities of human conduct. They also argued that social experience is the source of our characteristic moral feelings; and it was left to Dewey more than anyone else to explicate the status of values in nature.

All these analyses were carried out in great detail and their implications extensively explored. The findings in these inquiries have great significance for human well-being. They provide a charac-

Philosophy and Moral Values

terization of the nature of the situation of man in the world, including an accounting of its main limitations and resources. Thus, it became possible to identify means of functioning within this inclusive situation. In this task, modern philosophy had been ineffectual.

Notice that the philosophic conclusions to which I have adverted are not moral imperatives, nor do they entail moral imperatives. Yet they are extremely important in discriminating the human condition in a way which facilitates the efforts of individuals and groups to clarify, adjust, and unite their aims and to recognize the possibilities of an inherently precious experience. At the same time, the critique of erroneous moral theories liberates our thinking from fixation on beliefs which in fact limit or obscure our efforts to minimize suffering and enhance our well-being.

Dewey ceaselessly made recommendations for conduct. But it must be emphasized that they were recommendations; they made no pretense to be unconditional imperatives. He knew that it was within the powers of any knowledgeable and imaginative person to make recommendations, and that such proposals might turn out to be more congenial to persons in moral dilemmas than those offered by himself. He did not presume to legislate conduct. His intention was to point out the resources for human effort within the generic characteristics of the human situation. He attempted to make human beings sufficiently aware of their powers and their possibilities to permit them to cope with their problems and conflicts in a way that would unify their aims and enrich their experience. And he criticized moral systems and general philosophical systems for their failures to make perspicuous the nature of our situation and its potentialities.

What I wish to emphasize is that his contribution *qua* philosopher was to provide an accurate characterization of the world such that our human tasks could be effectively carried on in it, and to identify means for clarifying, criticizing, and pursuing these tasks.

Dewey, I believe, thought that this was all philosophy can do in respect to providing guidance for conduct. The elucidation of the human condition is no small matter, however, and his achievement therein accomplished much of moral value—more, indeed, than philosophers who engage simply in the attempt to specify criteria for determining good and right, or who simply analyze the logic of moral language.

It might be objected that if this is all the guidance Dewey's philosophy can provide, he has invited moral chaos—extreme moral relativism. This objection is premature, and I will not consider it explicitly until later. Let me here proceed to the second stage of the paper and summarize Dewey's main proposal for the conduct of life; namely, the adoption of social intelligence as moral method.

II.

On the basis of his analysis of the nature of the human situation, Dewey concluded that social intelligence is the most effective means at human disposal to discern and fulfill forms of life activity which are cherished in experience. He drew attention to the fact that our conflicts and difficulties arise in definite circumstances, which he called problematic situations. One of the most characteristic human desires is to convert situations of strife, doubt, and frustration into occasions of integrated activity, in which our human powers are effectively engaged and fulfilled. In Dewey's language, we typically desire to transform situations from problematic to consummatory.

All of us are more or less familiar with his analyses of the means of effecting these consummations: A situation presents many problematic values, and one attempts to conceive of an action which will combine and unify values which appear exclusive of one another. A hypothesis is formulated which specifies a course of conduct which will convert the situation into unified, or consummatory, experience. The specific action which is expected to integrate the situation is the end-in-view, and the integration of the situation itself is the consummatory phase of the entire process.

This much is familiar. What has not been well remarked about this procedure, however, is that Dewey conceives it as a *social* method.

Philosophy and Moral Values

Our moral problems arise when there are incompatible values in shared activities. Accordingly, the problem of transforming the situation is, in most instances, a social one, calling for the participation of several parties. The social method attempts to reconcile the conflict of values through the creation or construction of more inclusive values.

I will provide a bare outline of the nature of social method. Then I will give three main considerations for advocating it as a method for dealing with moral problems.

The method of social intelligence recognizes the starting point of the method in an actual situation where conflict or doubt has made further conduct problematic. A clash of moral commitments may well be involved. The parties to a socially problematic situation, if they subscribe to social intelligence, consult with each other to see if they can arrive at a hypothesis for redirecting their shared activity. If they succeed in doing so, and if their action achieves the predicted results, social intelligence has been effective.

Social intelligence brings conflict out into the open in situations where conduct is stymied and yet must go forward. As in no other method, it involves *communication.* When the parties to a problematic situation are wondering how they should behave in relation to each other, they do not deliberate by themselves, but they make moral discourse a public affair. A Kantian or neo-Kantian, by contrast, asks *himself* what he should do. This is really quite an odd procedure, especially when one professes respect for persons. When the other fellow's interests are involved, why not ask *him* what *he* thinks about the matter?

The parties can discuss what alternatives for action they can agree upon and can engage in together. Their discussion is also intelligent, in that the parties are aware of the nature of their circumstances and the intellectual and material resources available to them. They make an experimental inquiry into alternative ways of transforming their situation. They are also free, of course, to press for the values articulated in a particular philosophy. The convictions of Socrates, Hobbes, Hume, Nietzsche, Mill, or Kant can be urged for consideration and vigorously debated.

James Gouinlock

The hypotheses which predict consummatory situations contingent upon proposed actions are what Dewey quite unconventionally calls moral judgments.[8] They are not statements declaring that something is good, right, obligatory, etc., but they specify the means of reconstructing the situation; they predict a specific result. Clearly, then, they are empirically verifiable. When moral judgment is characterized in this way, it is clear why such judgments are scientific. Dewey takes for granted that individuals might subscribe to the truth of such judgments but might well decline to participate in a proposed action or even oppose it. There is nothing inconsistent about this: an individual acknowledges that such and such actions will have such and such results, but he finds these results unacceptable. Being scientific, then, is not going to solve all moral problems, and Dewey never supposed that it would.

We readily recognize that even in the most well-intentioned and cooperative persons, this method can hardly guarantee unqualified success, and in some contexts it will be hopeless. But for the present it is worth raising this question: *If* a moral consensus is to be attained by voluntary means, and *if* concerted action is to be achieved, how is it to be done? Dewey commented that the other methods had had their trial and were found wanting. Let us at this point consider more explicitly: Why social intelligence?

The first reason is that it earnestly recognizes the problems of moral disagreement as in no other decision procedure. Dewey repeatedly drew attention to the fact that the history of moral thought displays a remarkably diverse array of systems, and sincere moral practice displays a similar diversity. Given these facts, and given that we urgently desire means of living together, there are two alternatives open to us. The attempts can go on to formulate a moral system to which everyone with the wit to follow its arguments must assent. On the other hand, the attempt can be made to determine a means of carrying on human affairs in full recognition of the fact that conscientious persons advocate differing modes of action.

A philosopher enamoured of his own moral theory might well acknowledge that others will not agree with it, but—in his certitude— he might take the drastic step of believing that others must be trained to accept it. He can claim that his knowledge is available only to an elite, as Plato did, and on his own authority train people for their own good; or he can believe most of mankind to be morally corrupt, as Rousseau and Marxists have done, and be willing to force everyone along the right path. Such arguments, we know, are epistemologically bankrupt and/or question-begging. Yet they are tempting all the same. When others disagree with us, we are inclined to think that they are really not in a position to judge these matters as we are; they need to have the conditions of their judgment brought into line with our own. Needless to say, however, each of the rest is thinking the same thing about us; so the best thing to do might be to talk it over with them and be receptive to possible alternatives. If some of the contending positions are indeed freighted with ignorance, error, and invalid argument, the discussion can make this public.

If we wish to avoid being ruled by self-appointed moral absolutists, we would do well to recognize that moral disagreement must be approached in tolerant and social ways. Our intellectual and cultural history does not give us a shred of evidence that we can expect a universal consensus of moral values. It thus seems either naiveté or vanity for an individual to lay down moral norms to which he thinks everyone else ought to conform. The method of social intelligence commends itself precisely because it is an alternative to such absolutism.

Just as it guards against absolutism and takes moral disagreement seriously, it is also a remedy for extreme moral anarchism and relativism. This is the second reason for advocating social intelligence. Our conduct is carried on in a social medium, and like it or not—each of us must function with other people in the pursuit of our aims. Denial of this condition Dewey called an unnamed form of insanity.[9] Functioning in fact as a constituent part of a larger whole, a person can nevertheless attempt to act as an isolated atom. Such behavior will almost certainly result in frustration and defeat. Or he can deliberately attempt to act in concert with the whole, joining his powers with those of the rest. To do so, he must communicate with others and plan creatively with them.

James Gouinlock

The conditions of human existence are not such that anyone can act like a god. There are lessons to be learned about the limitations and possibilities of life experience. Not least of these is the knowledge of our social condition, with its sanctions and opportunities. There are lessons which can be widely learned and shared; and in fact they are, for moral problems arise out of the very conditions of associated life. No one has expressed with greater penetration than Dewey the continuities of social existence and moral behavior; and few have articulated a richer conception of the values of a community of shared experience. Such analyses make the lessons of experience explicit and emphatic.

Knowledge of the constraints and potentialities of particular situations is likewise conducive to the convergence of moral aims. Although social intelligence does not assure agreement on policies, a *shared* knowledge of the circumstances is an effective condition of a wider moral consensus. The method is explicitly public and informed; and because it occurs in the context of shared situations, it reveals that moral anarchy is not characteristic of intelligent behavior.

The third characteristic of social intelligence that commends itself to us is implied by what has just been said: it greatly facilitates the possibilities of individuals functioning together in a way that would enhance and fulfill their powers of activity. Social activity can be carried on simply in conformity with custom, by authoritarian procedures, or by ignoring the social nature of our existence. The two former procedures are not conducive to growth in individuality and freedom; they impose what Dewey called fixed ends. The latter procedure, complete individualism, is simply futile. Social intelligence, as a deliberately cooperative procedure, promises by contrast as much human development as this imperfect world will allow. There is no certainty, however, that social intelligence will produce harmony and happiness; there is no certainty that it will never be an instrument of oppression. But no means of moral thought and action can make such guarantees. The problems of human affairs simply do not admit of perfect solutions. "Perfect" solutions are conceived in the minds of philosophers, who have the conceit to impose their conceptions of perfection on others.

Patently, social intelligence is not something one can practice by himself. It is an inherently social process. If I try it and no one else does, my efforts come to naught. Dewey repeatedly urged that the habits of social intelligence be universalized. He says in the *Ethics*, for example, "The problem of bringing about an effective socialization of intelligence is probably the greatest problem of democracy today."[10] The most adequate test for Dewey's moral philosophy awaits such time as this socialization might occur. That is, the claims made for social intelligence are not to be tested by reference to theory, but in social practice.

Even without such a full-scale test, however, it is possible to observe merits of this pragmatic philosophy in comparison to some contemporary modes of analysis of moral issues. This brings us to our final topic.

III.

Not long ago, sophisticated philosophers were saying that ethics could not be a rational discipline in any sense whatever. They were succeeded by those who claimed the province of philosophy is to study the inherent "logic" of moral language. Many others, however, have thought this is a pretty meager conception of what resources intelligence can contribute to the moral inquiries and strivings of mankind. It is widely supposed, nevertheless, that the required breakthrough must involve a refutation of noncognitivism. I should like to suggest that Dewey's conception of the philosopher's competence in moral affairs does not provide grounds for the refutation of the theses of noncognitivism, but simply renders them irrelevant. These theses are all concerned with the logic of moral language, but Dewey's moral philosophy is unaffected by whatever this logic may turn out to be. Certainly the fundamental analysis of man and nature, which is of such great moral import, needn't be interlarded with moral expressions. And the discourse of social intelligence itself does not require the use of verifiable definitions of moral terms. I would argue that such discourse—although it performs a profoundly important moral *function*—can very well do without the use of an explicitly moral vocabulary. The hypotheses that specify the conditions of integrated activity would more likely than not to be rendered obscure, misleading, or simply emotive by employing typical moral language. I do not choose, however, to argue this issue. Suffice it to say that the pragmatic analysis of moral values is such that by comparison the endeavors of ordinary language analysis in ethics suffer acutely from the vice of defect. (If we take R. M. Hare's ethical theory, for example, we find no intimation that ethical discourse might attain a public level.)

More recently we have been presented with two highly acclaimed works in moral philosophy which suffer from excess. I refer to the works of Rawls and Nozick.[11] Each of these authors, I believe, qualifies as a moral absolutist. Each suffers from a kind of *hubris* regarding the competence of philosophical analysis to settle moral affairs. Each presumes to settle with finality certain moral problems. The fact that their systems are thoroughly incompatible with each other is indicative of the futility of such ambitions.

Rawls has tried to write the definitive and in some ways final book on the subject of justice. The invariant principles of justice will be determined by the parties to the original contract: the persons in the original position, with its uniform constraints, deliberate behind the veil of ignorance. These people are notably unlike the people of the real world: they are not individuated in any way whatever, they have no distinctive identity, and they have no prior moral commitments or social loyalties of any kind. Under these conditions of choice, it is assumed that they will finally be in complete accord in formulating principles of justice. Nothing less than complete accord is necessary to legitimate these principles.

The traits of the postulated beings in the original position are declared to be definitive of the moral person, and the individualized traits of real people are morally irrelevant. In this scheme, respect for persons is explicitly confined to individuals only insofar as they share the traits of the entities of the original position. In the same way, the moral judgment of ordinary human beings is not to be relied upon: moral truth is achieved only when our nature is denuded

Philosophy and Moral Values

and functions behind the veil of ignorance. If we were to deliberate with full self-knowledge, we might arrive at variant principles, and the desired uniformity of judgment would vanish.

The judgments of the beings in the original position are morally binding on the inhabitants of the real world. When the moral convictions, expectations, and loyalties of the latter conflict with the former, they may be completely disregarded. Rawls presents a final system, in which the criteria of all moral conduct are determined literally once and for all. It is a fixed moral universe, ruled by an abstract moralism, and not subject to any empirical test in social practice. If this system of justice worked out in the social world to be repugnant to the values of conscientious persons, so much the worse for those values.

Rawls, of course, says the principles of justice are what every one *would* choose if they thought their way into the original position, or its alleged equivalent, reflective equilibrium; so he even calls his theory democratic. But there are several difficulties in Rawls' reply: Would the choices in the original position be as he claims? Many critics have disputed his position.[12] Therefore, there is a genuine possibility of moral disagreement even under the conditions of choice specified by Rawls himself.

What is more important is that Rawls has contrived what he regards as the ideal conditions of choice; but this ideal is itself loaded with moral presuppositions, any one of which is controversial. Rather than isolate any particular one, let us consider only the fact that all the conditions of the original position are unlike those of the real world. Now then, what possible sense does it make to say that the choices in the original position are the ones *we* would make? We are the very complex people of the real world, and the beings in the original position are something else entirely. It is a contradiction in terms to say that *we* could be *them*. It remains inescapably true that the creatures of the original position are radically different from you and me. Therefore, if we disagree with the principles of justice, this is genuine disagreement, in no sense explained away by arguing that a different kind of being would accept them. And, indeed, many convictions about justice entertained by flesh and blood people are alien to those of the original position; yet, in Rawls' system, these people are nonetheless obliged to conform to them. This situation seems to be a consequence of Rawls' desire to establish perfect moral uniformity. But obviously at some cost to those persons with differing moralities! It is not by *their* choice that Rawls' principles are adopted, and Rawls doesn't even give the values of such persons any weight in moral deliberation.

We may with full moral integrity resist the sort of absolutistic morality that Rawls has demanded of us. And this is the crucial point. He has presented a theory intended to apply universally and to coerce universal consent among rational beings. If disagreement is possible, his system, as such, fails. We *could* choose to conform to it, of course, but Rawls gives us no compelling reason to do so. Rather than present his theory as an option to be evaluated by living people, he urges in Part III of his book that social institutions be arranged in such a way that everyone will learn to love this particular kind of justice.

Nozick's failure is of a similar sort: he has tried to accomplish what is beyond the competence of philosophy. Persons have absolute rights, he says, and that is the end of the matter. Thus, for example, any kind of taxation, regardless of its source and purpose, violates these rights. Consequently, no government, he claims, has any business in any sort of welfare activity. His claim is so absolute that the distinction between kinds of govermnent is wholly irrelevant. Even a democratic government is not entitled to levy a tax, say, to feed the children of incompetent parents. This is so even when a vast majority desires to make such assistance a matter of policy, rather than leave care of children to the vagaries of charity. It is so even when the minority opposed to the policy supports the decision-making process which yielded the policy and voluntarily abides by it.

We all know that a minority is offended by any democratic decision. Should they, then, preserve their absolute rights by withdrawing from this society? The fact is that they almost never have any serious desire to do so, because community life is precious. Society is a much more complicated affair than Nozick realizes.

Philosophy and Moral Values

A society enjoys a shared past, and its members anticipate a shared future. Its interdependencies are various and strong. It incorporates many values and loyalties. Unfortunately, these values and loyalties are not wholly compatible with each other. Nevertheless, the ties are typically much stronger than the conflicts. Communities can't be broken apart on every controversy, and no sane person wants them to be. Our moral commitment to a community is great enough that we tolerate many things in it that we prefer were otherwise. Actual human associations—from the family to the nation—could not otherwise endure. Hence there are ceaseless violations of what *Nozick* regards as inviolable. Virtually everyone in a community condones what *to Nozick* are immoral practices; but the social participants do so willingly, for they can't accept a morality which would destroy the values of community.

These are values of which Nozick appears to have little cognizance; but, like Rawls, he doesn't take it upon himself to consult the actual interests of human beings.[13] Evidently it would have no bearing on Nozick's philosophy if a community often valued some things in preference to these alleged rights, and was willing on occasion to sacrifice these rights in some measure.

Especially in light of Nozick's blunt admission that he hasn't any proof that we possess absolute right over our possessions, it is an odd morality that demands that millions dismiss their thoughtful moral values. Nozick says, in effect, that the procedures of social intelligence are profoundly immoral. Those of us who are interested in the endurance of society can be grateful that social issues are not typically approached with his implacable moralism. We can think of social intelligence as a precious ideal, not because it is morally obligatory, but because it answers to the needs, values, and intelligence of real people functioning in the real world.

In contrast to the inflexible moral categories propagated by both Rawls and Nozick, consider the following from Dewey's *The Public and Its Problems*:

...One reason for the comparative sterility of discussion of social matters is because so much intellectual energy has gone into the supposititious problem of the relations of individualism and collectivism at large, wholesale, and because the image of the antithesis infects so many specific questions. Thereby thought is diverted from the only fruitful questions, those of investigation into factual subject-matter, and becomes a discussion of concepts. The "problem" of the relation of the concept of authority to that of freedom, or personal rights to social obligations, with only a subsumptive illustrative reference to empirical facts, has been substituted for inquiry into the *consequences* of some particular distribution, under given conditions, of specific freedoms and authorities ...

The question of what transactions should be left as far as possible to voluntary initiative and agreement and what should come under the regulation of the public is a question of time, place and concrete conditions that can be known only by careful observation and reflective investigation.[14]

Readers of Rawls and Nozick will find some moral views in each which they find appealing: perhaps Nozick's entitlement theory of justice or Rawls' redistributive theory. Yet such readers will have no taste for either system as an invariant moral guide. They will find that in some circumstances they favor a decision by entitlement and in others by redistribution. Such readers would find themselves in a quandary, if they supposed their moral commitments had to follow from a self-consistent system of moral imperatives.

But morality needn't work that way; moral situations are often too problematic to be settled without ambiguity, doubt, and conflict. In his *Pragmatism and the Tragic Sense of Life*, Sidney Hook argues that the moral life as conceived by the pragmatists is inevitably tragic. There are irreducible moral conflicts: of the right and the good, the good and the good, and the right and the right. Hence there are no perfect moral solutions, and the moral response to one type of situation may well be different from that to another type. If, as Hook argues, the moral life is inherently tragic, we can understand why a person does not have to possess moral certainty in order to have a morally earnest and virtuous nature. Moral dilemmas are genuine. Intelligence, steadfastness, and good intentions are not enough to rid us of the tragedies of choice. Can any honest man assert that he never suffers from ineradicable moral perplexity? Yet such a man can have profound and unselfish virtues.

Philosophy and Moral Values

IV.

Does pragmatic social intelligence make the guidance of conduct an arbitrary affair? Does it make morals hopelessly relativistic? I have argued that it does not. Because of the persistent fact of moral disagreement, absolutisms exacerbate moral conflict and leave it without rational resources for creating agreement. Complete relativism is at the opposite extreme from absolutism: it despairs altogether of moral consensus and likewise of concerted behavior. To pirate the phraseology of Aristotle, social intelligence is the mean, but with regard to constructing shared values, it is an extreme.

When individuals are disposed to social intelligence, their possibilities for mutually supportive activity are enhanced beyond those provided by any other method. But they will not solve all their problems. That is an idle dream. And one may refuse to subscribe to the decision of social intelligence and may in fact conscientiously resist it. There is no moral law which says we must conform, and we should be grateful that there isn't.

If one is looking for a philosophic theory which will remedy our every moral dilemma, then he is bound to be disappointed. But this is a disappointment born of unrealistic expectations. We should not be critical of the philosophic enterprise for failing in that which is beyond human competence. At the same time, we may expect of philosophers that they clarify the nature of the human situation in order to identify its limitations and resources. Without issuing moral imperatives, and without constructing omnicompetent ethical theories, several pragmatists have made an enormous contribution to the moral enlightenment of mankind.

It is wholly within the pragmatic spirit that this sort of philosophizing be continued. In a like spirit, social intelligence should not be regarded as the last word in moral philosophy. Its problems, conditions, limitations, and uses must be explored. Alternatives to it should be carefully investigated. As I urged initially, further inquiry is needed to identify the various contributions that philosophy can make to moral intelligence.

James Gouinlock

The pragmatic tradition has demonstrated extraordinary competence in moral philosophy. It provides us with abundant resources for dealing with both theory and practice; and it challenges us to carry on in its methods and aspirations. Thus philosophy will participate in the main enterprise of human affairs.

NOTES

1. "The Will to Believe," section IX.
2. These are what Lewis calls rational imperatives. *See* esp. *The Ground and Nature of the Right* (New York: Columbia University Press, 1955), Ch. 5.
3. *See* esp. *Human Nature and Conduct* (New York: The Modern Library, 1930), pp. v-ix.
4. *Encyclopaedia of the Social Sciences* (New York: Macmillan, 1934), Vol. XII, pp. 118-29.
5. John Dewey and James H. Tufts, *Ethics* (New York: Henry Holt, 1932), pp. 175-76. All references in this paper to *Ethics* are to portions of it written by Dewey.
6. Dewey, *Ethics*, p. 365.
7. John Dewey, "Democracy and Educational Administration," *School and Society*, XLV (1937), pp. 457-62. Reprinted in part in Gouinlock (ed.), *The Moral Writings of John Dewey* (New York: Hafner Press, 1976), pp. 258-61. Quotation is from the latter, pp. 258-59.
8. *See* esp. *Theory of Valuation*, Ch. IV. *See also* Gouinlock, *John Dewey's Philosophy of Value* (New York: Humanities Press, 1972), pp. 299-314.
9. John Dewey, *Democracy and Education* (New York: The Free Press, 1966), p. 44.
10. Dewey, *Ethics*, p. 408.
11. John Rawls, *A Theory of Justice* (Cambridge: Harvard University Press, 1971). Robert Nozick, *Anarchy, State, and Utopia* (New York: Basic Books, 1974).
12. *See* for example, H.L.A. Hart, "Rawls on Liberty and Its Priority," *The University of Chicago Law Review*, 40(1973), pp. 534-55; David Lyons, "Rawls v. Utilitarianism," *The Journal of Philosophy*, LXIX (1972), pp. 535-45; Scott Gordon, "John Rawls' Difference Principle, Utilitarianism, and the Optimum Degree of Inequality," *The Journal of Philosophy*, LXX (1973), pp. 254-61; and Joel Feinberg, "Duty and Obligation in the Non-Ideal World." Ibid., pp. 263-75.

13. Nozick's method is to speculate concerning what *would* explain the state, *given the assumption of absolute rights.* He apparently is not interested in contending with the actual values that bring about particular institutions. See *Anarchy, State, and Utopia*, pp. 6-22. "A theory of a state of nature that begins with fundamental general descriptions of morally permissible and impermissible actions,... and goes on to describe how a state would arise from that state of nature will serve our explanatory purposes, *even if no actual state ever arose that way*." Ibid., p. 7.

14. John Dewey, *The Public and Its Problems* (Chicago: The Swallow Press, n.d.), pp. 192-93.

INDEX

Adams, H., 13
Alienation, 92
Analytic-synthetic distinction, 37
Anti-Pragmatist, 60
Ayer, A. J., 31

Behaviorism, 36
Bentham, J., 25
Biological evolution, 53
Brown, N. O., 74–82

Civil War, 11, 12
Cognitive growth, 53
Comte, A., 28
Condorcet, J., 7
Constitution of the United States, 10
Consummatory experience, 106
Contextual definition, 25
Continuity thesis, 51, 58
Crick, B., 52
Cultural pedagogy, definition of, 73

Darwin, C., 49
Democracy, 102
Dewey, J., 3, 15, 35, 37, 83–92, 101–12

Emerson, R. W., 9
Empiricism, post-Humean, 33; radical, 45
Empiricist tradition, 23
Enlightenment, 7
Enlightenment reason, 8
Epistemology, 46
Eschatology, Marxist, 81
Evolutionism: Quine's, 55
Experimental inquiry, 85

Frege, G., 26

Generic traits of nature, 89

Holism: Quine's, 55; relative, 27
Holmes, O. W., 11
Human nature, 103
Hypothetico-deductive method, 33

James, W., 3, 11, 15, 32, 35, 52, 58, 69, 100

Kant, I., 34

Lewis, C. I., 15, 34
Locke, J., 14, 24

Marcel, G., 44
Marcuse, H., 77–82
Marx, K., 49, 77; eschatology of, 81
Mead, G. H., 37, 100
Meaning, 18
Metaphysical Club, 10, 12, 15
Monism, methodological, 23
Moore, G. E., 101
Moral choice, 102
Moral judgments, 108
Moral method, social intelligence as, 102–17
Moral theory, competence of philosophy in, 99
Morris, C., 37

Naturalism, 28, 35
Nature, status of values in, 104
Neopositivism, 61
Neurath's boat, 28

Observation conditionals, 27
Ontology: Idealist, 35; Sensationalist, 30, 34

Index

Paradigm shifts, 45
Paraphrasis, 25
Peirce, C. S., 3, 5, 7, 15, 29, 32, 100
Perception, 45
Physical nature, 103
Plato, 14
Pluralism, 58
Popper, K., 43
Practical bearings, 29; reason, 15
Pragmatic conception, 18
Pragmatism: Critical, 17; definitions of, 50
Pragmatist, 60; Conceptual, 34
Pragmatists, Cambridge, 6, 11
Progress, 7

Quine, W. V.: evolutionism, 55; holism, 55; scientific method, 62

Rawls, J., 112
Realism, 34
Reality, 33
Relative holism, 27
Russell, B., 26

Schiller, F. C. S., 33, 43

Science, 15, 44, 57, 71
Scientific method, 5, 31; Quine's, 62
Scientific sentence, 27
Semantic primacy, 26
Semantics: behavioristic, 36, 37; Dewey's, 37
Slavery, 10
Social Darwinism, 49
Social intelligence as moral method, 102–17
Spencer, H., 15
Sri Aurobindo, 73
Syncategorematic, 24

Thoreau, H. D., 9
Thucydides, 14
Tooke, J. H., 24
Truth, 5, 31, 34, 55

Utility, 7

Verification theory, 31
Vienna Circle, 26, 30, 34

Weber, M., 62
Wordsworth, W., 7